KOREAN STUDIES SERIES No. 33

Interrelated Issues in Korean, East Asian and World Literature

Cho Dong-il

Jimoondang
Seoul

Jimoondang
514-7 Munbal-ri, Gyoha-eup, Paju-si, Gyeonggi-do 413-756, Korea
Phone: 82-2-743-0227 E-mail: edit@jimoon.co.kr
82-2-743-3192~3 E-mail: sale@jimoon.co.kr
F a x: 82-2-743-3097, 82-2-742-4657
Home page: www.jimoon.co.kr
ISBN 89-88095-98-7

The National Library of Korea Cataloging-in-Publication(CIP)
Interrelated issues in Korean, east Asian and world Literature/
by Cho Dong-il. -- Paju : Jimoondang, 2006
p.; cm. -- (Korean studies series ; No.33)
ISBN 89-88095-98-7 93800 809.9-KDC4 809.895-DDC21 CIP2006000574

Printed in Korea

Preface

I am studying the interrelation between Korean, East Asian, and world literature. On this theme I have published more than fifty books, but as most of them are written in Korean, they are not widely known and read. The contributions I wish to make in improving the global age are unfortunately trapped behind the language barrier.

Two books used European languages. *Korean Literature in Cultural Context and Comparative Perspective* (Seoul: Jipmoondang, 1997) presents some glimpses of my research. *Histoire de la littérature coréenne des origines jusqu'à 1919* (Paris: Fayard, 2001), written with Daniel Bouchez, shows an outline of Korean classical literature understood from a new viewpoint.

I have traveled widely to inform others of my discoveries and to find friends of common interests. I have attended many international academic conferences and given lectures frequently at foreign universities. The countries I have visited for those purposes are Japan, China, Taiwan, India, Kazakhstan, France, Switzerland, the Netherlands, Germany, England, Sweden, Russia, America, Australia, Egypt, and

South Africa.

The nine articles composing this book have been selected from the papers prepared for those conferences. Though varied in subject, they are reports of newly discovered interrelations among the literatures that have until now been considered irrelevant. The literary journey from Korea to East Asia, and from East Asia to the rest of the world offered me a precious opportunity to be a fortunate pioneer with unusual insights.

I would like to thank my companion Charles La Shure. He is an American student, now a Ph.D. candidate in Korean literature at Seoul National University. He continuously helped me to write better English. He is translating the massive volumes of my *Hangukmunhaktongsa* (*A Comprehensive History of Korean Literature*) into English. It will be very helpful in filling up the inevitable shortcomings of this small book.

New Year's Day, 2006
Cho Dong-il

Contents

I

Korean Studies in the Global Age

1

Distinguished guests and academic colleagues! Now we are attending an epoch-making academic conference. The international seminar for "Perspectives on Korean Culture," held here in New Delhi from October 7 to October 9, 2005, is an important milestone in the international development of Korean studies and in the friendship of our two countries of India and Korea.

This conference is officially sponsored by the Center for Japanese and North East Asian Studies of Jawaharlal Nehru University, which includes a Korean section. And this conference is actually planned, with the support of the Korea Foundation, to commemorate the 10th anniversary of the Korean studies programme and the 559th Hangeul Day. Hangeul, the Korean alphabet was created on October 9, 1446.

Such an unusual situation inevitably brings to mind the unhappy memory of Japanese colonial rule over Korea. Independence is an indispensable condition for the normal growth of a nation as well as an academic field. I do not like isolation, and want cooperation. But each must be free to realize genuine mutual understanding and aid.

2

Korea was one of the countries that lost its sovereignty and became a colony. The colonizer was Japan, a neighbour in the East Asian civilization sphere. This was a peculiar case. East Asia was a single civilization sphere with highly homogeneous and interrelated national cultures. When European powers invaded the whole world, the individual nations went their separate ways. Japan disavowed their membership in the East Asian civilization sphere and sought to join the ranks of the colonial powers. China became a semi-colony and suffered civil war. Vietnam lost its independence and became a colony of France. Korea was colonized not by a European nation, but by an old friend, Japan.

For this reason, Koreans were less fortunate than other nations in Asia and Africa that also suffered colonial rule. The modern knowledge of the West was introduced indirectly by way of Japan, making a deep understanding of it impossible. Japan failed to secure the moral superiority that would justify their colonial rule, and so enforced a military rule that leaned toward brutal fascism, utterly denying freedom of press or thought.

But Korea succeeded in inheriting two precious traditions: the high level of learning that originated with the East Asian civilization sphere and the creative variety of national culture. Putting these indigenous abilities to effective use, she obtained independence, modernized socially, and developed economically. That is the reason why Korea became the forerunner of Third World countries.

Korea is divided into North and South. The military tension is still strong. Though a milestone in the journey toward peaceful coexistence has recently been reached, there are still many difficulties ahead before reaching the goal of a unified Korea. As the political situation is gloomy, cultural abilities have to offer a hopeful perspective. It is the great duty of scholars of Korean studies to correct the distortions of culture wrapped up in politics, and to put forward a persuasive alternative view based on wide ranging, in-depth research.

Accumulating the results of extensive research, we scholars of Korean studies have to prove and make widely known the fact that the Korean people's long history and splendid tradition are the source of energy that will enable us to overcome the North-South division. While recognizing anew the homogeneity of the East Asian civilization sphere, we have to once again forge closer ties with neighboring countries. At the same time, we have to continue to clarify and discuss the ethnic differences and distinctive characteristics that have contributed to creating variety within this homogeneity. To achieve world peace and attain the kind of development of world history that we all wish to see, Korea has to go beyond pessimism by asking what East Asia can contribute from the viewpoint of idealism.

Currently, there is an argument going on over the assertion that Korea has to play a balancing role in East Asia.

In military terms, this is completely unthinkable. In terms of politics there are also many difficulties, and a consensus has still not been reached. The state of affairs on the Korean peninsula has given rise to an even greater degree of anxiety. But in terms of culture, the claim that Korea can play a balancing role is perfectly reasonable. In this case it is not only possible, but also convincing and desirable.

In the East Asian civilization sphere, China has been at the center, Japan at the periphery, and Korea and Vietnam in intermediary positions. Maintaining a close relationship with both the center and the periphery, Korea had a good understanding of the overall extent and structure of the East Asian civilization sphere and was able to map out a middle way that avoided extremes. By conducting proper research into these historical origins and by being aware of both the center and the periphery, we will be able to make a positive contribution to bringing unity to East Asia once again.

3

Korea is facing various international challenges these days, including Chinese claims on the history of Goguryeo and Japanese distortion of history textbooks, But narrow-minded national defence is a worn-out countermeasure. Korean scholars must have a universal world view to persuade scholars of Chinese and Japanese studies to move in a different direction. To awaken them to the fact that China's superpowerism and Japan's imperialism are impediments to scholarship, a more convincing view of history has to be developed.

To take this point one step further, we have to take up the task of expanding the field of comparative studies and establish a general theory that is applicable on a worldwide level. By going beyond nationalism toward universalism, we have to provide the direction that will lead all of mankind into the next era. Only Korean studies that are not *just* Korean studies are true Korean studies.

I have long conducted comparative research of Korean literature with the literatures of the other countries of East Asia—China, Japan and Vietnam—have obtained many meaningful and valuable results. If we are aware of the overall nature of East Asian literature, we can also clarify our understanding of the literatures of each country within the region. Furthermore, only by conducting comparative research into East Asian literature and the literatures of Europe and various other civilizations can we recognize their specific characteristics and speak with any authority about the entirety of world literature.

Comparative research is also necessary in order to discard our self-centeredness and come to an understanding of others. It's a big mistake to make the claim that globalization is an inevitable trend at this time while still pursuing the exclusive economic benefit of one's own nation or trying to transplant one's own values into another country. In order to correct this kind of mistake, we need to carry out genuine comparative research based on equality and a wide variety of perspectives.

Until now, comparative literature has tended toward microscopic studies and been devoted to proving relationships of influence. We now have to carry out macroscopic comparisons and make an effort to discover the points of difference and commonality in each independently established literature or culture. Comparative literature's most important tasks and goals must be to discard the bias of Eurocentricism, conduct research into the numerous literatures of the world from an equal viewpoint and illuminate the universal aspects and values of all of world literature.

4

Through broad comparative studies, I tried to find the Korean role in the global age. This is the answer. The most valuable contribution that the Korean cultural tradition can make is in the creative activity of harmonizing things that are essentially different in order to create new values. The wisdom that establishes harmony while acknowledging conflict and encourages growth while not denying antagonism is the best way of solving the countless problems that we face today.

On the basis of this principle, conflict is reconciliation and reconciliation is conflict. The idea that overcoming is becoming may be termed the "overcoming-becoming theory"(saenggeuk ron). The "overcoming-becoming theory" is the only way of expressing the term saenggeuk ron in English. The dialectic of the "overcoming- becoming theory" functions through the corrective tendency in "overcoming" to move toward "becoming."

We can ascertain the origin of this way of thinking in the

Silla period writer Choe Chiwon, who maintained that the profound Way (do) that existed in our country was also contained in Confucianism, Buddhism and Taoism. He stated that the manifestation and process of recreation that took place as a result of the fusion of our indigenous culture with Confucianism, Buddhism and Taoism was unusual and profound. In every age, figures such as Wonhyo, Iryeon, Choe Jeu and others established new systems of thought by absorbing cultures from various outside sources and recreating them by harmonizing them with the indigenous culture.

Husbands and wives, parents and children, and brothers and sisters, while believing in different religions and even engaging in arguments, still do not break off relations but continue to live together in harmony. From outside Korea, this is an amazing thing that is difficult to understand, but Koreans consider it to be completely natural. This kind of wisdom that is necessary for our future is appearing for the first time in human history and is now being tested in Korea.

Korean mask dances dynamically demonstrate the paradoxical idea that conflict is reconciliation and reconciliation is conflict both between the characters that appear in the performance and between these characters and the spectators. In other forms of Korean performing arts as well, the appeal of performances that make our minds feel comfortable even while they increase our feelings of tension has given rise to the phenomenon of the “Korean Wave” (hallyu), which is currently receiving a rapturous welcome in many countries in East Asia.

Let’s take a look at the Korean dish, bibimbab, which demonstrates a unique characteristic of Korea. The various ingredients, while continuing to exist in themselves, come together to form a harmonious unity, showing that overcoming is becoming and becoming is overcoming. New types of electrical products such as mobile phones, for example, are created in this way and are enjoyed all over the world.

5

Now the whole world is facing a crisis. In order for us to be able to go beyond the increasing conflict resulting from competition in the fields of science and technology, and economics and politics, the humanities have the mission of demonstrating the rationality of living in accordance with such ideals as the unity of the human race. That is to say, we have to go beyond the clash of civilizations and strive for their reconciliation and unity. The most valuable tradition of Korean studies is the wisdom of humanities.

The situation in the world today is such that while class conflict has been eased to some extent thanks to the positive contributions of technological and economic development, a different kind of serious conflict, namely ethnic conflict, has become even more severe. Because of these ethnic conflicts, blood is being shed in numerous places around the world, such as Northern Ireland, Palestine, Chechnya, Iraq, Afghanistan, Sri Lanka and Tibet. The mission and task at hand for the humanities is to carry out research into the true nature of the main causes of these ethnic conflicts, such as religion, language, customs and history, and provide a diagnosis for them and insights with which to solve them. If we doubt the value of the humanities, then the future of the world looks dark indeed.

Even though we have to continue to strive for the improvement of living standards and social equality, life's satisfactions, such as internal and spiritual fulfillment, which material development alone cannot provide, have to be provided by the humanities. From ancient times until the Middle Ages, the humanities held sway over scholarship. In recent times, the social sciences have split off from the humanities and have taken pride in their own independent growth, while the natural sciences have emerged to demonstrate their own power and push the humanities into the background. In order to go beyond the contemporary era and create a new era, the humanities have to come to the fore once again. It is the mission and task of the humanities to play the leading role once again in providing an overarching theory for all branches of scholarship.

The post-modernist idea prevailing in the West that history is coming to an end is a fallacy. There must be hope in the twenty-first century. We have to go beyond the conflicts of the present and create the next era that is more desirable. The Western philosophy of history, while recognizing the defects and limitations of the present age, has been unable to put forward any alternative. This is evidence of a failure of thinking. We cannot just stand by and watch while all that humanity has considered valuable up to the present, such as history, logic, values, and so on, is held up for ridicule and rendered futile.

We have to engage in rigorous scholarship, equipping

ourselves with sound logic and a proper set of values, in order to go beyond the present age and participate creatively in history as we go forward into the new era. The leadership role of the First World has come to an end, the opposition of the Second World has lost its effectiveness, and it is now time for the Third World to take the lead. In this regard, the cooperation between India and Korea is very important.

II

The Problem of Canon in Korean Literature

1

"Canon" is an English word that was unknown in Korea until recent times. Now it is frequently used, translated as "jeongjeon," among literary critics with a background of Anglo-American learning. It is not a pedantic term, but means rather simply the writings evaluated and recognized as standard or authoritative.

Such an idea is not new. The words "jeongo," "jeonmo," "jeonbeom" were used in traditional Korea with a similar meaning. In this paper, I discuss the canon of Korean literature as a succession to the heritages of our Korean forefathers.

Every civilization and nation has its own canons. The ideas and the methods of forming canons seem to be not so much different from each other. We can also identify a common process of rearranging canons. This will offer a key to world-wide comparison of the developments of cultural and literary history.

In Europe, the Bible or Holy Scripture was the first-tier of the canon, and the second-tier was comprised of Greek and Latin classics. English literature was only deemed fit to be evaluated as part of the canon in the 20th century. East Asian and Korean cases can be clarified in comparison with Western counterparts.

2

The Holy Scriptures of Confucianism were the highest canons of East Asia for a long time, when Confucianism was the universal ideal of all civilization. They were the *Analects, Mencius*, *Treatise on the Middle Way*, *The Great Learning*, *The Book of Odes*, *The Book of History*, and *The Book of Changes*. Classics of literature, such as Tang poems and Tang and Song prose, were ranked in the second-tier of the canon. Unlike Europe, these two tiers in their original forms used classical written Chinese. Religious, philosophical, and literary traditions were more closely related in East Asia than in Europe.

Beginning with the age of Southern Song, China no longer produced a common canon of the whole civilization. The other East Asian countries—Korea, Japan and Vietnam—competed with China by creating their own writings in written Chinese, along with vernacular literatures. Some eminent poets, such as Yi Gyubo in Korea, Setsgai Tsushin in Japan, and Nguyen Trai in Vietnam, adeptly expressed nationalist themes using written Chinese.

However, not only in Korea, but in the other East Asian

countries as well, national heritages of the literature in written Chinese were generally depreciated. They were sometimes added to canonical lists as third-tier, additional works. The hierarchical order could not be changed. But this was better than the situation in Europe, where Latin literatures produced in England or in the other countries from the medieval age and on were not deemed worthy of inclusion in the canon.

3

Two anthologies of Korean literature in written Chinese by Choe Hae (1289-1340) and Seo Geojeong (1420-1488) brought about a turning point in the recognition of neglected heritages.

In the preface to his anthology, *Easterner's Writings*, Choe Hae said:

> As we Eastern people's language is different from Chinese, if the talent inherited is not lucid and keen, strenuous effort in study can not win success [in producing the best work]. But just as the essence of mind [to be expressed in literary work] is the same all around the world, the satisfactory works of our writers are not at all inferior to theirs.

Seo Geojeong explained why he compiled *Anthology of Eastern Writings* :

> These are our Eastern nation's literatures, not Song

> and Yuan literature, nor Han and Tang literature, but our nation's literature. These works must live between heaven and earth with the (Chinese) literature of each generation. How they can disappear and be lost?

The best writers, whose works were given priority, if listed in chronological order, were: Choe Chiwon, Kim Busik, Yi Inro, Yi Gyubo, Yi Jehyeon, Yi Saek, Gweon Geun. Their works attained the level of the canon.

Some private anthologies of poetry followed. Heo Gyun's (1569-1618) *Selection of National Poetries* and Jang Jiyeon's (1864-1921) *Anthology of the Great Eastern Poetries* are good examples. These books boasted the achievements of Korean poetry in written Chinese.

Among the anthology of prose works, the final product was *The Prose of Nine Writers of Koryeo and Han(Joseon) Dynasties*, compiled by Kim Taegyoeng (1850-1927), while he was exiled in China. Kim Busik, Yi Jehyeon, Jang Yu, Yi Sik, Kim Changhyeob, Bak Jiweon, Hong Seokju, and Kim Maesun were selected as the nine best writers. The compiler wanted to let Chinese readers know that Korean writers created masterpieces on the same level as Chinese classics.

4

Vernacular literature in the Korean language was unable to shed its lowest status and rise to the level of the canon. But

Gyun Yeo's (923-973) hyangga works, "Songs of the Ten Wishes of Bohyeon(Samantabhadra) Bodhisattva" enjoyed an exceptional reputation, as it expressed the highest form of Buddhist thought, Choe Haenggwi an able writer of the same period, translated them into written Chinese. In the preface, he compared hyangga with the poetry in written Chinese.

> The sounds [of two songs of both countries] are distant as a star in the East and a star in the West. The ideas [of two songs] compete each other as a spear and a shield, and it is hard to determine which is superior. In competition, they will flow down together to the ultimate sea of truth, each taking it this own way. Why is this not good?

As hyangga disappeared, this theory could not be inherited by succeeding generations. When vernacular songs reappeared in sijo and gasa, they were regarded as playing a supplementary role to cover the shortage of poetry in written Chinese. Yi Hwang (1501-1570) and other poets, who showed creative ability in both domains, said that songs in Korean were indispensable for singing and dancing, and for moral purification.

Some eminent works, though, got a special reputation. Jeong Cheol's (1536-1593) gasa, "Special Song of Gwandong," "Song of Longing for a Beauty," "Second Song of Longing for a Beauty" are good examples. Kim Manjung (1637-1692) said that these three songs were "genuine literary works of Left of the Sea." "Left of the Sea" is a term for Korea. "Genuine literary works" means that their quality is excellent enough to be included in the canon.

Such an evaluation could not cover all of vernacular verse. In the 18th century, *Songs of Green Hill* and other anthologies of sijo works appeared with the declared mission of preserving them. But sijo and gasa were never regarded as more than subsidiary songs.

Prose works in Korean were not considered literary works. Though vernacular novels were produced abundantly and read widely, they were denounced as harmful to morals. But Kim Manjung's novels, *The Dream of Nine Clouds* and *Lady Sa's Journey to the South* received special appreciation for two reasons: the author was a well-known high-ranking officer, and the two novels have philosophical and moral meaning.

5

The first modern *History of Korean literature* (1922) was written by An Hwak. He wanted to treat with equal importance the two domains of Korean literature, the literature in written Chinese and the literature in Korean, and clarify their mutual dependency. But it was only a rough outline that lacked the necessary details. Unfavorable circumstances during the colonial age hindered further achievement.

Cho Yunje's *History of National Literature* (1949) was the product of liberated Korea. It made great advances in its use of materials, and it had a systematic framework. It was accepted widely as a reliable text book, not only in universities but also in high schools. In this book, Cho Yunje defined Korean literature based on a nationalist ideology. He turned the classical hierarchy of the two domains of Korean literature upside-down. The literature in written Chinese was degraded to a marginal level, and the literature in Korean came into focus.

Among the writers of the literature in written Chinese regarded as producers of the canon by classical anthologists, Hong Seokju and Gim Maesun were omitted. The reason is that Cho Yunje thought they had no noticeable relationship to the main current of Korean literary history that had been newly described. Some other important writers of the literature in written Chinese were mentioned in relation to vernacular literature.

Works of the vernacular literature in Korean, already evaluated, were welcomed as heroes of literary history. Hyangga and sijo were praised as precious expressions of national spirit. Jeong Cheol's (1536-1593) gasas and Kim Manjung's novels became model masterpieces in the canon. *The Story of Hong Gildong*, *The Story of Chunhyang,* and some other well known popular novels were added to it.

This is not a final conclusion. During the recent half century, the study of Korean literature has developed tremendously. Many neglected works were found and analysed. The Bongsan Mask Play, Gim Ryeo's poems in written Chinese dealing with social reality, and *Banquet of the Coverant Under the Moonlight* the longest Korean novel ever at 180 volumes, are typical examples. To accept new members, the established canon system must be reconsidered.

Furthermore, a new view of literary history is needed. I

wrote my *A Comprehensive History of Korean Literature* (the first edition in 1982-1988, the fourth edition in 2005), in 5 volumes, to carry out such a demand. The main points of my attempt can be summarized as follows.

There are three literatures in Korean: oral literature, literature in written Chinese, and written literature in Korean. They had equal importance. They competed and intermingled with each other. The literary historian has to clarify that process with a broad perspective and deep insight.

The distinction between major and minor works must be abolished. The contributions of the lower class and women must be recognized with a new insight. Oral narrative songs, which are transmitted and recreated by shamans, lead to the rediscovery of a lost vein of ancient literature. Ordinary vernacular letters of women, excavated by accident from old tombs, are precious proofs of literary life.

The scope of literature is broadened extensively, and replaced by new conceptions of the text or of literacy. The conception of canon loses meaning and is disappearing. Now I am writing the fourth edition of this book to be published in 2005. It will manifest the anti-canonical direction more clearly. That is one of the most important tasks in overcoming the modern conception of literary history.

6

We can identify three stages in the history of the canon in the Korean case. They were closely related to intellectual and social history.

Classical canons of the common written language of the whole civilization ruled for a long time when the universal idealism was the leading ideology. These were then replaced by the canons of vernacular literature, in the age of the modern nationalism of the 20th century. Now the conception of the canon is questioned and distrusted, with the goal of creating a new type of egalitarian society.

The Korean case demands a detailed investigation and comparison with other countries near and far. We are now at the starting point of a long journey. If the same process is found through a good amount of meaningful evidence all around the world, it will contribute much to proving the unity of human experiences.

Two Korean Vernacular Epics of the 15th Century

1

Korean literature is peculiar in that it has many epics. The oral epics transmitted as shaman songs are similar to the traditions of the Ainu in Japan and minority peoples in China. The written epics in classical Chinese, such as the famous poet Yi Gyubo's *Saga of King Dongmyeong* (*Dongmyeong-wangpyeon*, 1193) (hereafter referred to as *King*) and the Buddhist monk Unmok's *Eulogy of the Acts of the Buddha* (*Seoggayeoraehaengjeoksong*, 1328) (hereafter referred to as *Buddha*), have no equivalent in other East Asian countries.

When the Korean alphabet, called the "Proper Sounds for Teaching the People" (*Hunminjeongeum*), was invented in 1443 and begun to be used officially in 1446, written epics in the Korean language appeared. *Songs of Flying Dragons* (*Yongbieocheonga*) (hereafter referred to as *Dragons*) and *Songs of the Moon's Impression on a Thousand Rivers* (*Wolincheongangjigok*) (hereafter referred to as *Moon*) were written in the same year, 1447. Chinese and Japanese literatures do not have such works.

King Sejong, the fourth ruler of the Joseon Dynasty, invented the Korean alphabet and tested it for the first time by writing epics. That means that for a long time there was an unrealized desire to have written epics in the Korean language. He ordered those who collaborated with him in inventing the alphabet, Jeong Inji and Gweon Je, to write *Dragons*. He read its manuscript and gave it its title. He himself composed *Moon.*

2

Dragons was the dynastic epic needed for a national policy that established the political ideology. The founding heroes of the new kingdom were praised as dragons. The Buddhist epic *Moon* was written as an expression of the king's own personal faith or the faith of his family. The moon symbolized the enlightened Buddha giving love to all living creatures.

The prior example of a dynastic epic is Yi Gyubo's *King.* Although *King* sung of ancient history in written Chinese and *Dragons* treated recent history in the Korean language, they embodied the same tradition of praising the heroes who played the leading roles in Korean history. And both of them depicted the great deeds done to establish a political ordered that benefited the ruled peoples as much as possible.

The two epics are the product of medieval universalism, but their ways of realizing it are different. *King* used written Chinese, observing its rules of versification. *Dragons* first described the deeds of the ancient Chinese kings idealized by Confucianists and then compared them with native heroes. In *King*, linguistic universalism coexists with nationalism. In *Dragons*, the ideological universalism of Confucianism is the other side of linguistic sovereignty.

The life of Buddha was covered in numerous Buddhist scriptures, and the Indian poet Asvaghosa wrote an epic of adoration in his *Buddhacarita*. Other countries in East Asia were satisfied with the written Chinese translation of this work, but Korea wrote two new Buddhist epics. The first was Unmok's *Buddha*, composed in written Chinese, and later *Moon* in vernacular Korean. This was due to a unique interest in epics on the part of Koreans.

The messages of the two Buddhist epics were different. *Buddha* sought to widely teach the proper attitude of faith to those living in the end times spoken of in Buddhism. *Moon* offered Buddhism as the solution to the internal agony that Confucianism, the ideology of the new era, could not solve, thus making it the complement to *Dragons*.

Dragons and *Moon* were written as soon as it became possible to write songs in Korean because both Confucianism and Buddhism, official life and private life, the exterior and the interior, and this world and the next were equally important. Both sides had many things to say and were waiting for a way to express them. The two vernacular epics manifested Korean recreation of the traditions accepted from two centers of great civilizations, China and India.

3

Dragons is a poem that praises the achievements of the founding ancestors and the establishment of the Joseon Dynasty. By writing and singing a song that revealed that the nation was founded with the support of the people, those in the royal court were convinced of the legitimacy of the dynasty and instilled with a sense of duty. It was also vital to sing this song and influence the hearts of the people.

When *Dragons* was sung aloud, the music it was sung to was called *Being Merry with the People* (Yeomillak). This name was given in the hope that its influence would extend to the people and that they would share in the enjoyment. After the Japanese Invasion of 1592, *Dragons* was republished, indicating that this intent was not forgotten by future generations.

In order to gain the trust of the people, it was necessary to accept oral tradition. They could not stop at accepting various tales that dealt with the founding of the nation, but needed to approach the deep place where memories of the national foundation epics lay dormant. It was there that they needed to come into contact with the long tradition of the national culture. In carrying out the task of embodying Confucian ideology, they asserted that the founding ancestors of the Joseon Dynasty were on an equal level with the ancient kings of China. What they created was a Korean vernacular national foundation epic that accomplished both of these goals.

The full text consists of 125 cantos. The first canto is one line, and all proceeding cantos are two lines each, with the exception of the last canto, which is three lines. The first two cantos are as follows.

Canto 1

The six dragons of the land east of the sea fly up; all their works are blessed by Heaven, and are just like those of the ancient sages.

Canto 2

A tree with deep roots is not moved by the wind, but bears good flowers and much fruit.
The water from a deep spring does not dry up in a drought, but forms a stream and flows to the sea.

The theme of the entire work is summarized here. The six dragons of the land east of the sea, a term used to refer to Korea, are King Taejong, King Taejo and his paternal ancestors going back four generations. It boasts of the long history of this family, which had pushed as far north as the lands of the Jurchen (Manchuria), and their eventual establishment of a dynasty, and deals with the history of six generations so that the ancestors may be exalted by the glory of their descendants.

The image of six dragons flying up to the heavens borrows symbolism from the Chinese *Book of Changes* to express their ascendance to the royal throne. This is the meaning of the poem's title. The poem goes on to say that they were blessed by heaven and accomplished a great task, just like the sages of old, and it uses metaphor to say that they will continue to prosper because their foundation is firm.

Of the three fundamentals of heaven, earth, and man, the first canto deals with heaven. The second canto deals with earth, and the rest of the poem is the domain of man. Heaven is one line, earth is two lines, and man extends over a number of lines, but in the last canto of the poem it is three lines. This shows the process of realizing the principles of heaven, earth, and man by increasing the number of lines.

The central part from canto 3 to canto 109 shows the trials and struggles of the hero used in the various ancient national foundation epics, praising the founding of the new dynasty. Although it does not incorporate the idea that the hero's birth was out of the ordinary, it sings of the trials and life of wandering suffered by the first four generations, followed by the founding of the dynasty through King Taejo's dazzling ability, and then the process by which King Taejong accomplished what remained of the task. The life of the hero is substituted with the history of a family, producing a national foundation epic that spanned a number of generations. Let us take a look at a few important passages.

Canto 22

He slew the black dragon with one arrow and saved the white dragon, and the divine creature foretold the auspicious fortune of his descendants.

Canto 83

By a measuring stick institutions are born; that he may rule benevolently, Heaven sent down a golden measuring stick.

The white dragon and the black dragon were fighting with each other, and the white dragon asked King Taejong's grandfather to kill the black dragon. In canto 22, King Taejo's grandfather slays the black dragon with one arrow. There are similar stories all over the world. The epic gives the defeat of the dragon as the best example of the hero's ability, and tells how the grandson carries on the great work begun by his grandfather.

Cantos 63 through 89 praise King Taejo's character and introduce symbolism to show that the foundation of the dynasty did not happen by chance. Canto 83 explains that a measuring stick is needed to establish the system of rule, so the heavens gave Taejo the golden measuring stick so that he might rule wisely. It is only natural that there are such signs when a dynasty is founded.

The golden measuring stick has a dual function: it guarantees royal authority and sets the standard for establishing the system of rule. Measuring sticks are used to measure distance. Only by precisely measuring distances can all institutions be properly established and can the king control himself and rule appropriately. The age was gone when a nation could be controlled by military might alone, and thus the golden measuring stick was introduced to emphasize the importance of excelling in both civil and military matters.

Cantos 110 through 125 are the conclusion of the work and a request to future kings. It asks them to remember the difficulties of their forefathers and not forget their purpose when they founded the nation, and it warns them against bringing about the ruin of the nation through mistakes in ruling. It tells them not to enjoy a life of peace and luxury, making punishments their sole activity, forgetting virtue in their arrogance, listening to the crafty and exploiting the people. It concludes with the statement that the essence of government is the ruler observing his own standards of conduct, not commands given to the ruled by the ruler. We can see by this that it considered future kings to be its most important audience.

4

Moon is an epic that sings of the life of Sakyamuni Buddha. It was written in three volumes, but only the first volume and an incomplete version of the second volume have been discovered. The cantos that remain number around 410. It is thought that the entire work consisted of around 580 cantos.

The title of *Songs of the Moon's Impression on a Thousand Rivers* is from a simile that compares the Buddha's appearance in ten billion worlds and his preaching to the moon shining on a thousand rivers. Just as there is only one moon, yet there are countless manifestations of it as it shines on the rivers of the world, so it is for the Buddha, and so it is for humanity. The Buddhas of the ten billion worlds are not different from each other. The numerous people on the earth are bound by their own karma and thoughts, but their thirst for the Buddha is the same. Based on this symbolism, the song begins as follows:

> *Canto 1*
> Though taking eons, who can speak of all the unfathomable and unending virtuous deeds of the lofty glorious one?
>
> *Canto 2*
> I will speak of the works of the holy Buddha, and although they happened far away, look at them as if you could see them with your eyes.
> I will speak of the works of the holy Buddha, and although they happened one thousand years ago, listen to them as if you could hear them with your ears.

In the first verse, the narrator wonders how it would be possible to speak of all the deeds of Buddha, which cannot be known and have no end. Yet that does not mean he will be silent. There is a way to approach the Buddha, and that is revealed in canto 2. The holy Buddha mentioned in canto 2 refers to the historical person of Sakyamuni, whereas the glorious one mentioned in canto 1 is the Buddha of ten billion worlds. Even though the deeds of Sakyamuni occurred far away and one thousand years ago, the narrator tells the reader to consider them as if they were visible to the eye and audible to the ear.

Space and time are divided into three levels. The virtuous deeds of the Sakyamuni Buddha are limitless in both space and time. The actual words and deeds of the historical

Buddha are distant in both space and time. However, since the narrator sings of these words and deeds now, they are close in both space and time. He writes a song about what can be seen and heard right now, in order to ensure that the Buddha's teachings will last for all eternity.

From the third verse on, the song speaks of the historical Buddha. The narrator sings of the experiences of the historical Buddha as he lived countless past lives, beginning an unfathomable number of eons ago. He drastically expands the scope of time, relating events that exceed the imagination. When he comes to describe the events that took place around the time that Sakyamuni achieved enlightenment, transcendental things and everyday things coexist in an interesting contrast. The dual nature of Sakyamuni is highlighted: he is an ordinary person, yet he is also the enlightened Buddha. In this way, both the narrator and the audience can personally identify with Sakyamuni, and at the same time discover anew the reason why he should be worshipped.

Let us take a look at the scene were Sakyamuni returns to his hometown after his enlightenment to meet his father, the king. Here, a person named Utaya appears. Utaya was sent by Sakyamuni's father to find his son, but he became a disciple of Sakyamuni and returned with him. All three of them had much to say.

Canto 115

Utaya tells of having finally achieved enlightenment
after practicing asceticism for countless eons.
The father replies that, after twelve years, he finally

hears this today.

Canto 116

The king told what happened long ago, and Utaya and his son listened.

But he did not know what had happened recently, so Utaya and his son told him.

In canto 115, Sakyamuni's companion Utaya tells the king of how Sakyamuni practiced asceticism for many eons and only now has been enlightened, and his father the king says that after longing for his son for twelve years he has finally heard news of him. Many eons and twelve years, the joy of enlightenment and the joy of meeting one's son are contrasted with each other. In canto 116, Utaya and Sakyamuni listen as the king tells of what had happened when Sakyamuni was young, and Utaya and Sakyamuni tell him of what had happened recently. As the son is the Buddha and the father is an ordinary person, they of course have different things to say to each other upon meeting, but they agree in that they are both happy. Utaya is also happy to have reunited a father and son and brought together an ordinary person and the Buddha.

5

There is also an interesting contrast in the composition of the stories. *Dragons* spans six generations, telling of the trials and struggles experienced by each generation and ultimately the great achievement of founding a new dynasty, while *Moon* tells of a single individual, the Buddha, who was reincarnated, experienced trials, disciplined himself, and finally achieved great enlightenment. They are the same in that the many become one and trials end in glory and praise. At the same time, they are different in that the relationship between the many is different. The level of glory that is achieved is distinct in each story. In telling their own stories, they complement each other.

Dragons excluded commonality in it its attempts to depict a world of heroes unattainable by ordinary people, but in *Moon*, Sakyamuni, who had achieved a high state of enlightenment, was also an ordinary person who lived an ordinary life that anyone could experience. The father-son, mother-son, and husband-wife relationships in Sakyamuni's life were depicted much as any other relationship. His father the king is an ordinary person who sorrows at parting and looks forward to their next meeting. When his son says that he will follow his father, who is now the Buddha, his mother weeps bitterly. All the suffering of life, no matter what kind, is depicted in a touching manner. There is a separate, lofty world that transcends suffering.

Both epics opened different ways for the literature of future generations. *Dragons* was similar to the heroic trials and struggles of the protagonists in later novels. *Moon* was structured in such a way as to deal with the relationships between transcendental principles and common reality, and lofty ideals and ordinary experiences.

III

Korean Literary History in the East Asian Context

1

From 1982 to 1988 I published the first edition of *Hanguk-munhaktongsa* (*A Comprehensive History of Korean Literature*, which covers the entire development of the history of Korean literature. This was revised and published in a second edition in 1989, and revised and published again as a third edition in 1994. Much time has passed since then, and the task of rewriting it once again cannot be put off. I plan to publish the fourth edition at the beginning of 2005, adopting newly discovered materials and integrating the results of the latest research.

When I first wrote this history of Korean literature, I focused on the development of the history of Korean literature itself and did not deal with its relationship to foreign literature. After achieving my planned task, I then set about verifying in a variety of ways how the principles and facts I uncovered in my description of Korean literary history could be applied to East Asian literary history, and how much they contribute to a new understanding of world literary history. The results have been published in the following books. All books are written in Korean. Here I present the titles translated into English.

A Comparative Theory of East Asian Literary History (1993)
Fiction and Facts in Writing World Literary History (1996)
Catharsis, Rasa, Sinmyeongpuri: Three Principles of Drama and Film (1997)
Aspects and Changes in East Asian Oral Epics (1997)
One and Many East Asian Literatures (1999)
Common Written Language Literature and Ethnic Language Literature (1999)
Similarities and Differences in Civilizations (1999)
The History of Philosophy and the History of Literature: Two or One? (2000)
A Comparative Study of the Social Histories of the Novel (2001)
The Development of World Literary History (2002)

Going as far as summarizing the development of world literary history, I was able to confirm that my history of Korean literature made a proper beginning in its inquiry into literary history. A good start made it possible to go a long way. I researched a proper understanding of the division of periods in literary history, the interrelation between oral literature, common written language literature, and national language literature, and the fact that the history of literature is tied up with the history of other fields, even correcting misconceptions concerning the history of world literature.

I wrote the fourth edition with the results of this new research. But I can not present all of them. What I can do in this paper is to explain some important items that are most vital to an understanding of the history of Korean literature in the East Asian context.

2

The first era of Korean literature was that of oral literature. The first important genre of oral literature, national founding epics, showed characteristics typical of ancient literature. When national foundation epics were no longer made and "hanmun" (classical written Chinese) appeared, there were great changes in the structure of the class responsible for writing literature. In order to write hanmun, one had to diligently study writing. Being a writer was reason to boast. Yet it was not an age in which writers could express themselves in their writing. They were technicians, writing what their government ordered them to write.

The adoption of hanmun and the creation of a hanmun literature was unfortunate in that it caused the egocentric literature expressed in the Korean language to be relegated to the province of lower-class culture, where it struggled against the dominance of hanmun literature. However, this transition from the ancient era to the medieval era, where the common written language and world religions of one's civilization sphere are adopted, is a common process that occurs in any developed nation. In this way, humanity is able to share its wisdom, experience social changes that overcome the isolation, inequality, and illogic of the ancient era, and advance both ideologically and artistically.

Common written languages did not destroy or overrun ethnic languages. As ethnic languages were unified, consolidated, and developed into written languages, they developed the ability to express high culture. The modern sorrow at the loss of many native words or grammatical forms due to this development is of no help in understanding the actual historical circumstances. No nation has been able to cultivate an ethnic language into a national language without accepting a common written language. We should not envy the Philippines or Sub-Saharan Africa. They suffered the aggression of modern Western powers without the cultural background of a national identity and were forced to use the language of their aggressors as their official language.

We can argue over whose ancestors played the leading role in achieving the common written language and world religions of a particular civilization sphere. We can lament the fact that our Korean ancestors could not achieve these on their own, even though they were very active in scholarship. This way of thinking, though, is born of modern nationalism. Medieval universalism considered all the property of every world empire to be in the public domain. We should not be applying a modern nationalist concept in an attempt to determine the ethnicity or nationality of certain medieval world empires. It is an even greater mistake to deny the existence of civilization spheres and divide them into ethnic nations.

We would be mistaken to view the medieval era in East

Asia as a vast empire founded by the Han people of China. Even when the Han Empire emerged as the ruling order of a unified China, they had not yet reached the medieval era, but were still in the transitional period from the ancient era to the medieval era. This is because they were still preparing a common written language and universal religion. When different peoples from the north established their empires in the middle reaches of the Yellow River, there was a cooperative effort to realize medievalization by forces both within and without China. A turning point was the transformation of written Chinese into a common written language and the establishment of Buddhism, both of which were accomplished within China by Northern Wei and without China by Goguryeo.

A number of dynasties followed in the north and south, and the countless peoples who participated in the process that led to the Sui and Tang Empires engaged in a cooperative effort to enrich medieval civilization. These fruits were adopted and developed further by various other nations, creating an East Asian civilization sphere. In terms of nations, the initial members of the East Asian civilization sphere were the various dynasties of China, Nanchao in southwestern China, the three kingdoms of Korea (Goguryeo, Silla, and Baekje), and Japan. The family grew even larger with the addition of Vietnam, which freed itself from long domination by China, and the Ryukyu Islands, which underwent a late medievalization.

The publicly owned properties of medieval civilization cannot be considered the private possessions of any one ethnic nation. This mistake is not made in other civilization spheres.

Only in East Asia has the medieval world empire—that is, China—continued to the present day, so the medieval era and the modern era have become confused. The history of literature must actively help distinguish that which has been confused, making it clear that the medieval era is the medieval era, not the modern era.

In the medieval era, there was a distinction between the "son of heaven" and the king. "Son of heaven" is a literal translation of the term used in the East Asian civilization sphere, "cheonja" in Korean, "tianzi" in Chinese, to refer to the earthly representative of the heavenly deity. The title is equivalent to the caliph of Islam and the pope of European Christianity. Because the son of heaven was the sole agent on earth of the highest deity worshipped by an entire civilization sphere, there could only be one son of heaven (or caliph, pope, etc.) in each civilization sphere. Only then could the son of heaven undertake the role of connecting heaven and earth, guaranteeing homogeneity within a civilization sphere and clearly establishing the foundation of political order or virtue, thus preventing chaos. The ancient custom of a king wielding the authority of the gods of heaven still remained in some places during the medieval era, but these cases are not convincing enough to negate medieval universalism.

A king's sovereign power was only justified if he was invested with his title by the son of heaven. In places where a distinction was made between the son of heaven and the emperor, the son of heaven invested the emperor with his title, who then in turn invested the king with his title. The relationship formed by such investiture of titles had religious and spiritual significance, but was not a political lord and vassal relationship. It would be a mistake to say that the land ruled by a king was not a sovereign nation. The emperor symbolized the spiritual sovereignty of the whole civilization area, while a king symbolized the political sovereignty of his country. The medieval era was an era of dual sovereignty. In cases where rulers below the king were autonomous, it was an era of triple sovereignty.

The common written language played an indispensable role in firmly establishing this view of order. The diplomatic documents exchanged by the emperor and king were among the most high-toned and ornately embellished documents composed in the common written language. The form and style were standardized, verifying the homogeneity of members of the same civilized world, and superiority and inferiority within that world were determined by minute differences in the methods of composition. Every ruling class author within that civilization sphere's territory could write the same forms of poetry and prose. Even if they could not communicate verbally when meeting, they could still communicate through writing.

Hanmun is not a spoken language, but a written one, and each country had a different way of pronouncing it, making it more heterogeneous than other common written languages. The differences in word order and grammar between hanmun and the Korean language were a constant cause for concern. When hanmun became the official written language, our ancestors did not express disapproval, but toiled long to devise a written language for Korean using hanmun. There were writing systems that wrote hanmun according to the Korean word order. There were also attempts to transcribe the Korean language using hanmun.

The medieval era was the era of hanmun, but hanmun did not dominate every aspect of life. Another characteristic of medieval civilization was the dual structure of hanmun: the original structure and the structure used to express the Korean language. This dual structure was magnified with the appearance of the Korean writing system of hangeul, and was finally overcome with the advent of the modern era.

3

The civil service examination system tested the ability to compose hanmun literature. Hanmun was very hard to study. But that examination was open to anyone not of humble origin and chose personnel for government service based on a test of ability. The civil service examination system was put into practice in China in 589, Korea in 958, and Vietnam in 1075. It was not put into practice anywhere else, giving these three countries a lead in East Asian medieval civilization. Japan maintained their old custom of appointing personnel to government posts according to status, and thus they fell behind and were relegated to the periphery of the civilization sphere for quite some time.

It is a mistake to criticize the civil service examination system, saying that it was improperly administered and gave rise to abuses. In those societies without a civil service examination system, government positions were decided by military struggles or hereditary status, and scholars and writers—like those of Silla—were relegated to the position of working level technician, no matter how skilled they were. As with all original ideas of history that have epochal significance, the positive contributions of the civil service examination system gradually decreased as its negative applications began to make themselves known.

Only when demands for the dissolution of the civil service examination system had grown fierce did the Europeans arrive in East Asia. They were shocked to discover an idea that they had been unable to think of themselves, and used this in belatedly establishing a modern examination system. The countries of East Asia, with Japan in the lead, have adopted the European examination system and are criticizing the civil service examination (despite the fact that they still implement it), but this is putting the cart before the horse. The civil service examination system, which led to the modern examination system, is important evidence in proving the superiority of East Asian civilization.

The most salient difference in the medieval East Asian civil service examination system and the modern examination system styled after the European model is in the subjects tested. Literature and law are the primary subjects, with the former being a literature examination and the latter being a law examination. In the literature examination, law was considered a secondary subject, used in selecting low-level personnel for administrative work. In the law examination, literature was considered to be of no use at all, and was excluded entirely.

If asked which was more important in ruling a nation, literature or law, a modern person would say law without hesitation. The medieval East Asians, though, thought differently. One must know humanity in order to rule a nation, they would say, and literature is best suited to the task of understanding humanity. All peoples in the medieval era felt that literature was not an ornament on the margins of life, but the most valuable of all human endeavors, and in East Asia this common conception was most clearly expressed and systematized.

The civil service examination was a literary examination because literature was valued over the practical affairs that moved society according to laws, and because it developed the mind, allowing people to comprehensively judge facts. If we discuss the issue again from the legal aspect, using the terms "positive law" and "natural law," natural law was considered to be above positive law, and it was felt that a desirable society could only be achieved if literary figures, who were the best judges of natural law, guided the experts in positive law. The ideal that a philosopher should rule the nation was realized, with literary figures taking the place of philosophers.

Literature, which was necessary to the civil service examination system, was not the literature of ethnic languages but of the common written language. The literature of the common written language was a means of communication used throughout the entire civilization sphere, and it offered a measure by which cultural levels could be compared. Based on the common scriptures, it also fostered a communal understanding of humanity and values, brought people closer together in terms of sensibilities, and offered the knowledge necessary in everyday life, such as knowledge of laws and institutions. In order to prevent the written language from being swept away by the spoken language and allow it to protect the common heritage, composition methods were strictly consolidated, individual differences were reduced, and the changes of the times were rejected. This was an amazing development at first, but gradually became conservative and led to abuses that became customary.

4

The literature of Korean language appeared with hyangga, which used hyangchal, a writing system that borrowed Chinese characters. Hyangga had a long history that began in the Silla period, but with the end of the early Goryeo period it disappeared. In order to uncover the reason for and meaning behind this fact, we must understand the greater current of literary history in relation to the tendencies of history in general.

In the early Goryeo period, the lineage aristocracy that carried on the traditions of Silla were responsible for upper class literature while they reigned as the ruling power, so hyangga was perpetuated. With the Military Officers' Uprising in 1170, the ruling system of the lineage aristocracy collapsed, along with all the support that would guarantee the survival of hyangga. The long period of early medieval literature had ended.

In the late Goryeo period, powerful aristocratic families ruled the nation, and the new literati grew as a competing power. The powerful aristocratic families had survived the

Military Officers' Uprising and the Mongol invasions, and during continued interference by Yuan China they seized an unusual opportunity to gain power and land, but they did not have the ability to rebuild upper class literature. They encouraged the king, who only sought pleasure and excitement, they relieved ideological tension, they cared nothing for dignity, and they enjoyed folk singing and dancing. The new literati realized that this would lead to the collapse of the nation, and so they sought to establish an ideology that would reform the ruling system.

In order to correct the fundamental wrongs of the ruling class, who trampled on the lives of the people and abandoned themselves to hedonism, a fundamental change in the way of thinking was required. The new literati were originally local functionaries and thus had a close relationship with the common people and handled all sorts of affairs, but a new world view was required that went beyond their experience: a world view that properly understood reality, made moral principles clear, and understood these two, reality and moral principles, as a unified whole. This meant proposing an alternative to the early medieval philosophy of the mind that was established by highly advanced theoretical Buddhism, and this had to be carried out in a number of difficult steps.

Reforms in the basic aspects of literature accompanied these changes in philosophical thinking. These changes in literature did not follow any precedent, but were wholly unique, and the basic task the new literati set for themselves was the creation of a new branch of literature. Only by understanding that the history of philosophy and the history of literature are at once separate histories and a unified whole can we understand this fact. Literary branches are the products of their ages and concrete realizations of ideology are vital to understanding the history of literature. Having confirmed this, we must go beyond the scope of literary research.

The hyangga had internalized the world by embodying the ideology of an age that placed importance only on the mind, but in the age when both the material and the way were considered important, a didactic poetry that globalized the self had to be newly established and a lyric poetry that internalized the world had to be recreated. For Korean language poetry, a unique creation that did not rely on foreign precedents, the early medieval era was the age of lyric poetry, while the late medieval period was the age when the lyric poetry of sijo and the didactic poetry of gasa coexisted. This is the clearest way of distinguishing between the early and late medieval periods.

This was not only true for Korean literary history. Vietnam was also an intermediate nation in the hanmun civilization sphere, and so they created late medieval didactic poetry in almost the same way as Korea. If we broaden the scope of our inquiry, we can see that intermediate nations in a number of civilization spheres all developed ethnic language didactic poetry around the 13th century: the Tamil in the Sanskrit civilization sphere, the Persians in the Arabic civilization sphere, the French in the Latin civilization sphere, and so on. It is also widely confirmed that such central nations as China already had a didactic poetry, while peripheral nations like Japan either had no didactic poetry or did not deal with issues of philosophy in song and poetry.

The form of thought that placed importance on both the mind and the material can be found in every civilization sphere, and it caused a simultaneous introduction of the late medieval period around the world. There were even basic similarities in the division of responsibility concerning the methods of embodying this change. A great teacher, such as Zhu Xi of China, emerged in the center of the civilization sphere and completed a common written language text that revised and systematized the fundamental principles of the common religion (be it Confucianism, Hinduism, Islam, Christianity, etc.) to include a recognition of the material. In the intermediate areas, which were unable to do this and thus fell behind, the cultivation of an ethnic language didactic poetry that expressed a new understanding of reality was offered as an alternative, leading the development of literary history. Nations in the periphery were in no condition to enter the competition.

The specific aspects of late medieval ethnic language didactic poetry are different for each country. In Korea, the didactic poetry of the late medieval period were Gyeonggi-style songs and gasa, and the lyrical poetry was sijo. Gyeonggi-style songs appeared first, and with their decline gasa become the dominant didactic poetry. Gyeonggi-style songs were short-lived, but gasa enjoyed a long life, playing an important role in the next era as well. Sijo are still around today.

5

The late Joseon period, after the Japanese Invasion of 1592, was the first stage of the transition between the medieval era and the modern era. The efforts to ensure the continuation of medieval literature and the movement to establish a modern literature were intertwined in a relationship of conflict and harmony; it would be a mistake to call this period an extension of medieval literature, and it was would be unreasonable to call it the starting point of modern literature. The transitional period between the medieval era and the modern era was not merely a transition, but an era that had its own distinct characteristics. There were two such periods: the transitional period between the ancient and the medieval era, and the transitional period between the medieval and the modern era.

The transitional period from the medieval era to the modern era cannot be given a concise, unique label, and we have no choice but to define its characteristics by referring to the dual character of medieval and modern literature, since the three-fold system of ancient, medieval, and modern is considered the starting point for the division of historical periods. We cannot, however, begin to describe the development of literary history by revising this three-fold system. It would be wiser to realize that reality is more important than terminology, and to view the revision of the three-fold system not as a prerequisite but as a result of the task at hand.

The Japanese Invasion of 1592, which lasted for seven years, was a severe trial that forced appalling suffering on the

Korean people, shaking the nation to its foundations. "Righteous armies" rose up around the country and reinforcements arrived from Ming China to repel the invaders. About a generation later, another disturbance occurred, this time in the north. Having founded the Later Jin Empire in 1609, the Jurchen (Manchus) eventually established the Qing Dynasty in China in 1644. Along the way they invaded Korea twice, once in 1627 and once in 1636, forcing Korea to suffer the humiliation of defeat. The Jurchen and Japanese had been regarded as little more than inferior barbarians, and yet when they overran the civilized nation of Korea, the ruling class had no means of coping with them.

Having exhausted their strength fighting in Korea, the government of Japan collapsed and was replaced by the Tokugawa Shogunate, and the Qing Dynasty replaced the Ming Dynasty as the ruler of China. The Joseon Dynasty, though, was already two hundred years old and showing its limitations, and although it suffered a decisive wound, it did not collapse but extended its lifespan for about another three hundred years. The excellency of the Joseon Dynasty, which was a model late medieval nation for not only East Asia but the entire world, acted as an impediment to historical development.

It was very fortunate that Korea was able to overcome the trials of the Japanese and Mongol invasions, but opinions vary on why this was possible and what it means. Those who say that loyalty was absolute said that it was only by the aid of heaven that the king did not pass beyond the borders of the nation and the royal line was preserved. If we think of the dynasty and the people as separate, though, even though the ruling system of the dynasty was showing its limitations both internally and externally, the people were still capable and could thus repel the foreign invaders and protect the cultural community. When the ruling class weakens, it is only natural that a critical and creative force should rise up from the lower class. As seen in the "righteous armies" that arose during the invasions, the lower class grew and their resistance intensified.

Suffering two wars and then entering into the transitional period from the medieval era to the modern era was a change that the three East Asian nations experienced together. Japan and China did not enter the modern era with the change in dynasties. However, while the Tokugawa Shogunate and the Qing Dynasty both established ruling systems appropriate to the transitional period from the medieval era to the modern era, effectively preventing the progression into the modern era, the Joseon Dynasty refused to abandon the ideals of the late medieval era and thus lost the ability to control society and aggravated the social contradiction.

No matter what the place, the most important social change of the transitional period from the medieval era to the modern era was the emergence of a bourgeoisie class that made their living through commerce and industry. This was also the period when the demands of the bourgeoisie for a change from a status-based society to a class-based society were rejected and the status system protected, leading to the coexistence of status and class. Qing Chinese society became one in which only those who passed the civil service examination were allowed to retain the highest status, while all others merely belonged to a class and had no status. The Tokugawa Shogunate bestowed on its bourgeoisie the status of chyounin (lit. "townspeople"), thus reestablishing the status system.

The Joseon Dynasty at first attempted to preserve the status system intact. When the bourgeoisie gained yangban status, though, followed by wealthy farmers, the majority of the population came to have yangban status and the status system became powerless. The ruling class, which failed to understand that a more fundamental change was taking place, tried to heal the wounds of war and divert domestic criticism by proclaiming that the Joseon Dynasty was indeed the last bastion of medieval values against the barbarians of Japan and Qing China. For this reason, even some cultural movements that sought modernization had to accept these values as their basic premise, and their thorough objections were either made with great effort or grew violent.

The numerous records, testimonies, recollections, and imaginings from all walks of life that arose from war brought the history of Korean literature to a new stage. Faced with a severe trial, writers abandoned formalities that they had respected up until then and sought new ways of vividly expressing that which they had seen, felt, and lamented. This was the case with everyone, and so the gap between the upper and lower classes was narrower than it had ever been before. This was the starting point of the literature of the transitional period between the medieval era and the modern era.

Even the historical records or journals left behind by government officials carrying out their official duties report in detail the course of the war and the events after it ended, moving the reader with their realistic depictions of the wretched scenes and their expressions of grief. Their experiences were so new that they could not explain them, so they needed to make an unprecedented attempt to simply describe what they saw and felt. Such attempts were published in hangeul (the native Korean script) as well, proving that the usage of hangeul had increased.

With the emphasis on expressing sentiments, poetry was chosen in favor of prose. Even in hanmun poetry, which followed traditional forms, the writers were not in a position to refine their writing, so they put content first. In sijo and gasa, there were cases where the authors failed to bring to life the experiences and sentiments themselves, and thus relied on ancient events and introduced moralistic explanations into the text. In tales and novels, authors could only use those types that had been handed down.

Old rhetorical methods were at odds with the new experiences, and this problem took a long time to solve. In cases where the goal was to reaffirm medieval ideology, harmony was achieved by either reducing or watering down new experiences. When questions about the overall meaning of life were asked, even without a drastic departure from the old rhetorical methods, the discord of form and content actually had a positive significance. Shaping the logic of the new experiences themselves into the structure of the work was possible from the literature of the very lowest class.

6

The novel took its place as the literature of the transitional period from the medieval era to the modern era. What had previously been called "novels" were no more than the pioneering works of outsiders that were ahead of their time. The novel gained its own distinct form and grew in earnest as a new literary genre during the transitional period from the medieval era to the modern era, the late Joseon period (17th century and on). At the same time, the age of the novel was beginning in other East Asian nations and in Europe as well.

In order to understand the beginning of the age of the novel, we need to examine the history of the changing era as the structure of philosophical thought and literary genres meshed. As philosophy changed, a corresponding change occurred in literature as well, so this change can be explained through philosophical concepts and logic. It is a fact that the history of philosophy and the history of literature are both separate histories and a unified whole everywhere in the world, but in Korea this fact is particularly clear.

During the medieval era, the universe was understood to be a duality of the mind/the way/the principle reason and the material/the vessel/the material force. In the early medieval period the distinction was between the mind and the material: the mind was considered genuine while the material was considered false, and so lyric poetry, which expressed the mind, occupied the highest position of all literary branches. In the late medieval period, the mind was called "principle reason" and the material was called "material force." They were both considered important and raised up side by side, establishing a structure of thinking that enabled the coexistence of lyric poetry and didactic poetry.

In the transitional period from the medieval era to the

modern era, principle reason and material force were considered at once separate and inseparable, but the theory of the duality of principle reason and material force was dominant, holding that material force was the more important. The theory of the monism of material force refuted this, and held that principle reason was merely the principle of material force and did not exist separately. This philosophy corresponds with the novel, which expresses the conflict between eum and yang (yin and yang) in the realm of material force as the conflict between the self and the world in the fictional work. In the structure of the novel as well there are elements which follow the dualist theory and elements which follow the monist theory, leading to controversy surrounding the retrogression toward the medieval era and the progression toward the modern era.

The novel succeeded the tale, but displayed the inverse of its relationship between the self and the world. It overcame the tendencies of the legend, which asserted the supremacy of the world in the conflict between the self and the world, and the folk tale, which asserted the supremacy of the self in that same conflict, and established a serious structure of conflict characterized by mutual supremacy. The novel is markedly different from legends and folk tales, which were oral literature that were occasionally recorded, in that it was created as written literature. Literary composition methods could not be borrowed from the tale, so a separate model was needed. That model was the biography (jeon). In name and form, the novel paraded as the biography, transforming the didactic into the narrative, fact into fiction, instruction into entertainment, and support of the ruling ideology into criticism of it.

The mission of the biography was originally to judge the rights and wrongs of individuals in their biographies in historical records, seeking to instruct later generations. Then there arose personal stories that, unlike official biographies, anyone could write, and the content and expression in these stories became more free, producing works that drew closer to the novel. There are works that could be called intermediate works that show an overlapping of the biography and the novel. This does not mean, though, that the novel was a later modification of the biography. The novel was a rebellious child, disguising itself as the biography, plagiarizing its method of narrating people's lives, and gradually usurping the authority the biography had enjoyed. Not only in Korea, but in other East Asian countries as well, the novel began as a "mock biography," just as it began as a "mock confessional" in Europe.

The relationship between the biography and the novel becomes the standard by which historical eras are divided. The period when there was only the biography and no novel continued through the early medieval era, and then the situation changed with the advent of the novel. The period during which the novel, which had been rejected because of its inferior position, posed as the biography was the first stage of the transitional period from the medieval era to the modern era. The reversal of positions in which the biography lost its influence and disguised itself as the novel was a change that occurred during the second stage of the transitional period from the medieval era to the modern era. In the modern era, the biography was excluded from the domain of literature and the novel wielded great influence.

The novel appeared and grew at the same time in each nation in East Asia, so a comparison is necessary. Through such a comparative study, a number of questions about the Korean novel may be answered. The Korean novel was greatly influenced by the Chinese novel, and there were not a few translations and adaptations, but their basic characters were different. This is a difference that is best examined in relation to social history, rather than literary theory.

The transcribing and, at the reader's discretion, adaptation of novels whose authors were unknown was something that only happened in Korea. In China, it was customary for an author to publish books under a pen name. In Japan, publishers requested manuscripts from authors and clearly stated the author's name when publishing these manuscripts, thus allowing them to maintain their popularity. It could be said that the novels of China were writers' novels, the novels of Japan were publishers' novels, and the novels of Korea were readers' novels.

Chinese novels, even those that were written in baihua, the colloquial language, could only be read and enjoyed by learned men. Japanese novels, which used kana (the vernacular script), were men's novels because of the characteristics of the content, not the language in which it was written Korean novels, though, were read mostly by women and actively addressed women's interests, and it is surmised that there were a significant number of novels written by women as well.

7

Modern literature is the literature of the period from 1919 to today. The literature of the period from the 17th century to 1918 is the literature of the transitional period from the medieval era to the modern era, divided into the first and second stages by the year 1860. In 1860, "Eastern learning" was founded and a collection of Eastern learning songs was published, ushering in a new stage of the transitional period from the medieval era to the modern era. With the March First Independence Movement in 1919, the transitional period between the medieval era and the modern era ended and modern literature began.

As we enter the period of modern literature, the relationship between Korean literature and world literature increases dramatically, demanding a wide-ranging comparative study. In studying modern Korean literature, we must keep in mind the fact that the basic character of modern literature is the same everywhere, only the timing and the process by which modern literature was achieved differ. Compared with the literature of the preceding transitional period, modern literature differs in the following aspects.

During the transition from the medieval era to the modern era, Eastern Asia was one civilization sphere that produced a homogeneous and interrelated literature, but in the modern era the individual countries each went their separate ways. Japan renounced its Asian heritage, joined the ranks of the European imperialist powers and devoted itself to aggression. China suffered civil war in a semi-colonial state, and there was severe ideological conflict in literary composition as well. Like Korea, Vietnam became a colony, but its ruler was France. Unlike most other nations in Eastern Asia, Korea was colonized not by a distant European power, but by its own neighbor.

For this reason, Korea was at a far greater disadvantage than other colonized nations in Asia and Africa. Firstly, modern Western literature was introduced second-hand by the Japanese, making a deep understanding of it impossible. Secondly, Japan was unable to secure the moral superiority needed to justify its colonial rule and thus enforced a military rule that leaned toward fascism, engaging in oppression that denied freedom of the press or of thought.

The first disadvantage seemed to be a difficult one to overcome. In terms of literary criticism, the indirect transplanting of modern literature did cause difficulties. However, in terms of actual literary composition, authors, whether they realized it or not, succeeded in carrying on the tradition of Korean literature and tapping into the wellspring of modern literature to create a national literature that may serve as a model for the Third World. The second disadvantage led to the misfortune of Korean writers having almost no creative freedom. Korean writers had to develop their literature differently than China, which went no further than a semi-colonial state, not to mention the colonial ruler of Japan. These two characteristics, though, did not cause literature to wither, but became a catalyst that led to a more faithful manifestation of the universal values of modern literature.

In Japan, writers who did not want to cooperate with the aggressors, but were oppressed for their proletarian literature and had genuinely abandoned the ideology of Communism, sought to create a literature that pursued sensibilities, as in the West. In China, literary critics who severely discussed the political ideology of the proletarian literary movement assumed leadership of Chinese literature. Korean writers were secretly inclined toward a proletarian literature that was oppressed more harshly than in Japan and linked this with the national literature. They eschewed the slogans of struggle and focused on composition, using indirect methods such as allusion, symbolism, and satire to criticize colonial rule and express their desire for national liberation. Although they did not proclaim it, they took on the duty of leading the people, earning great trust.

In poetry, the surface chaos that resulted from following the Japanese adaptation European literature did not go very deep. There were those who sought to revive sijo and others who insisted that poets should follow the Japanese precedent and write free verse. Yet there were also those who leaned to neither side, but inherited and modified traditional rules of versification and manifested in their poetry the national resistance against Japanese imperialism. The exceptional works produced by Yi Sanghwa, Han Yongun, and Kim Sowol were widely loved and considered a proud heritage of national literature, the likes of which cannot be found in either Japan or China.

Yi Yuksa and Yun Dongju, who died in prison toward the end of the colonial period, did not attempt to become political poets. Nor were they nationalistic poets. They merely expressed in simple lyrical poetry the desire to live truthfully and without shame, unconquered by the darkness of the age, and for this the Japanese government put them in prison and left them to die, making them martyrs for the cause of national liberation, proving that they had transcended such justifications as political ideology or nationalist consciousness.

The modern novel was established by Yeom Sangseop, and his *Three Generations* (*Samdae*, 1931) presented an unbiased a cross-section of the differences in ways of thinking and the severity of the struggle between ideologies that emerged along with the changes of the times. In Gang Gyeongae's *The Problem of Humanity* (*Inganmunje*, 1934), tenant farmers who could not bear the extortion of the landowners moved to the city and became factory workers, where they engaged in a bitter struggle with the factory owner. She depicted the typical process of proletarian struggle beneath colonial rule through a weak female protagonist and a style that showed a delicate sensibility. In *Muddy Stream* (*Tangnyu*, 1937), which carried on the tradition of pansori, Chae Mansik depicted the fate of one poor woman who could not deal properly with harsh reality because of her kind heart, alluding to the coming awakening of the people.

After liberation from colonial rule, Korea was divided north and south, and the writers of each side were cut off from each other and created different literatures. In the South, critics who claimed that the new currents of thought in European literature should be adopted were very influential, while in the North the goal was socialist realist composition. Both sides, though, attempted to write narrative poems and historical novels that would stand as monuments to national history.

The Medieval Age in Korean, East Asian, and World Literary Histories

1

When I wrote the five volume *Hangukmunhaktongsa* (*A Comprehensive History of Korean Literature*) (the first edition was published in 1982-1988, the fourth and most recent edition was published in 2005)[1], it was not easy to formulate a general scheme for the work. Listing relevant materials in chronological order was not sufficient. Theoretical argument was indispensable from the outset.

I seriously examined the popular periodization that consists of the ancient, medieval, and modern ages. Its defects are plain to see: as a Eurocentric conception, it may distort the histories of other civilizations, and, as it is cultivated and promoted in social history, it neglects the autonomy of literary history.

A proponent of so-called "total history," Marc Bloch recently reaffirmed that the medieval age was the feudal society that divided power and land.[2] He also insisted that only Western Europe and Japan honourably passed such a stage.

Scandinavia was mentioned reluctantly when it had undeniable relations with the core of Europe.[3] The other civilizations were not considered. Such a one-sided theory makes the situation worse. The hope of a universal understanding of world history seems to be a fantasy.

The periodization of the ancient, medieval, and modern ages explains only a specific aspect of world history, and without any convincing results. What is the common characteristic of the literary products of those two societies, Western Europe and Japan, that divided power and land? There is no answer forthcoming.

One way to avoid such an absurd universalism is isolationism, that is, to write each nation's literary history within its particular framework. Most works of national literary histories prefer to use indigenous terms which refuse to be translated into other languages.

This is not a desirable solution. There are two fatal defects in it: various doctrines of isolationism conflict with each other without any reasonable solution, and the hope of a general view of world literary history disappears. Then literary historians will not be able to defend themselves against the accusation that they are the most retrogressive, narrow-minded, and nationalist of all academic researchers.

2

I was determined to find a new starting point. That is to define the ancient, medieval, and modern ages in the context of

Korean literature and to test the validity of this definition in East Asian and world literary histories. The criterion I used was not social history but linguistic change. The key concept in my definition of the medieval age is diglossia, the relation between high and low languages.[4]

When the common written language of East Asia, classical Chinese ("hanmun" in Korean, "kanbun" in Japanese, "hanvan" in Vietnamese) was adopted as a high language in Korea, and the stage of diglossia began. This was the medieval age. Medievalization[5] was more clearly manifested in linguistic history than in other histories.

Before that time there was only oral literature. That was the ancient age in Korean literary history. In the modern age, diglossia was abandoned, and the former low language, vernacular Korean, took the place of the official language and became the national language. An understanding of such changes leads to a very simple, clear, and useful way of periodization.

The introduction of classical Chinese was accompanied by ideological change.[6] Official recognition of Buddhism in 372 was an important landmark, and Confucianism followed. From that time on, classical Chinese played an indispensable role in religious and political life. The monumental inscription at the tomb of king Gwangaeto (whose name means "the opener of wide territory"), made in 414, is a good example of an early literary work using classical Chinese.

Written literature in the Korean language began with songs inscribed in Chinese characters. The writing system was called hyangchal ("native writing") and the literary genre was hyangga ("native song"). "The Song of the Comet," composed by master Yungcheon (whose name means "coordinator of the heavens") in 594, is the earliest known example. From 1446 literature in the Korean language was written in the newly made alphabet *Hunminjeongeum* ("The Proper Sounds for Teaching the People").

During the long medieval age, high language — classical Chinese — and low language — vernacular Korean — produced different literatures. But themes and motifs were used interchangeably. Yi Gyubo, the 13th century poet, used classical Chinese to write a national epic recreating the tradition of a nation-founding myth. The leading neo-Confucianist of the 16th century, Yi Hwang, composed his sijo works, a type of lyric poetry, in vernacular Korean with philosophical themes.

There were many translations between high and low literatures. The interrelationship between the two literatures is an everlasting and fruitful field of study for Korean literary historians. Such experiences help open a new horizon for understanding literary history in a wider scope.

The balance between the two literatures was changing. During the first period, which I call the early medieval age, high literature dominated low literature. In next period, the late medieval age, which began in the 13th century, there were noticeable attempts to promote low literature. In the age of the transition from medieval to modern literatures, from the 17th to 19th centuries, low literature flourished and made high literature approach its level.

To clarify the sub-divisions of the medieval age, I added a second criterion of periodization, the change in literary genres. In ancient literature, the oral epic was the most important. But the dominant genre of medieval literature was lyric poetry.

In late medieval literature, the lyric poetry sijo coexisted with the didactic poetry forms of Gyeonggi-style poetry and gasa. Gyeonggi-style poetry is rather short stanzaic verse and gasa is rather long verse without stanzas. In the age of the transition from medieval to modern literatures, the canons of existing genres were shaken and a new genre, the novel, appeared.

Changes in literary genres were related to social history, especially to the replacement of literature-creating groups. When the warriors' hegemony passed on to the intellectual aristocrats, the lyric got the leading role instead of the epic. Newly emerged literati with realistic world views created the didactic poetries of the late medieval age. Beginning with the age of the transition from medieval to modern societies, the newly emerging bourgeoisie contributed much to promoting the novel.

3

What I have said so far can be summarized in four propositions: (a) written literature began in the medieval age; (b) the coexistence of high language — classical Chinese — and low language — national vernacular — is the characteristic of medieval literature; (c) the dominant genre of medieval literature was lyric, but in latter medieval literature lyric poetry coexisted with didactic poetry; (d) in the age of the transition from medieval to modern literatures, the canons of existing genres were shaken and a new genre, the novel, appeared.

Can these propositions be applied to the literatures of other East Asian countries, using classical Chinese as the common written language?[7] I selected China, Japan, and Vietnam as representative examples of East Asian countries. The result of the investigation is as follows:

	China	Japan	Vietnam
(a)	−	+	+
(b)	+	+	+
(c)	−	−	+
(d)	+	+	+

Vietnam has 4 + and no −, just like Korea. In (b), Vietnamese authors using classical Chinese produced not only national but also anti-Chinese works, best exemplified by the works of Nguyen Trai. In (c), Vietnam had the didactic poetry fu, similar to Korean gasa. The two poetic forms dealt widely with living experience, moral problems, and practical knowledge.

Japan has 3 + and 1 −. (c) is −, as there was no didactic poetry in Japan. There is also a speciality in (b): national vernacular literature played an important role the from early medieval age. The Japanese waka produced more abundant works than the Korean hyangga. *The Tale of Genji* also exemplified that tendency.

China has 2 + and 2 −. (a) is −, as Chinese written

literature began in the ancient age. So in (b) the distinction between languages is not clear. The literature using low language, baihua, developed later. (c) is −, as the Chinese didactic poetry fu appeared before the medieval age. Though Chinese fu and Vietnamese fu have the same name, their historical positions were quite different.

My theory can be said to have gotten 9/12 (3/4) approval in East Asian literatures. Now it has become possible to have a common periodization of East Asian literature, through which each nations' specialties can be closely compared. Such a result suggests that a general theory of world literary history may be possible.

4

Classical Chinese was not a unique common written language. Other civilizations also have their own common written languages: Sanskrit in South and South-east Asia, classical Arabic in West Asia and North and East Africa, and Latin in Europe.

Just as classical Chinese was the vehicle of Confucianism and Buddhism, the other common written languages were used respectively as the official medium of the religions of their civilizations: Sanskrit for Hinduism and Buddhism, classical Arabic for Islam, and Latin for Christianity. Common written languages are the most distinctive mark by which civilizations were divided.

The era of the common languages was the medieval age

in world history. During that time, from approximately the 4th to the 19th centuries, the diglossia of high language literature and low language literature coexisted in a large part of the world. It ranged from Japan in the East to Morocco in the West, from Iceland in the North to Madagascar in the South. In such homogeneity we can best see the unity of world literary history.

Unity does not exclude diversity. Innumerable literary works have their own peculiarities, and it is impossible to make a general theory comprising all of them. But such diversity is not chaotic. With a macroscopic view, we can identify much of this diversity as systematic transformations of this unity.

The relationship between the unity and diversity of literary history can not be identified in any single national literature. I tested it by comparing East Asian literatures. The results achieved in one civilization have to be compared with the other civilizations. This is the best way to formulate a general theory.

China's characteristics, written literature beginning in the ancient age and low langage literature developing later, were well manifested in the central parts of other civilizations. Also in the cases of Sanskrit, classical Arabic, and Latin, the homelands of the common written language lagged behind in vernacular literature.

Japanese national vernacular literature played an important role from the beginning of the medieval age, and this was a common trait of the peripheries. Java, Swahili, and Scandinavian literatures showed similar achievements. It is quite natural that among Scandinavian countries, the most remote country of Iceland was the best pioneer of national vernacular literature. The Icelandic saga[8] led medieval national vernacular literatures all around the world.

The problem of didactic poetry needs more detailed investigation. Not only classical Chinese but also Sanskrit and Latin literature produced many written works of didactic poetry in the ancient age.[9] That is the characteristic of civilization centers.

Japan did not participate in making didactic poetry, so the lyric completely dominated the domain of poetry. Such an exceptional tendency similar to the modern conception of poetry can be said to be a peripheric choice. It is necessary to find other literatures to compare with the Japanese case.

Korea and Vietnam are situated in the intermediate area of East Asian civilization, between the center and the periphery.[10] There are many other countries, also in the intermediate area of their respective civilizations, that eagerly wrote didactic poetry in the vernacular. Tamil, Persia, France and Germany are good examples.

Their vernacular didactic poetries offered new insights into the problems of understanding and evaluating living conditions that were impacted by the center. That was the most valuable achievement of late medieval literature. The age of the transition from medieval to modern literatures continued this trend and broadened its scope.

Newly emerged literati with realistic world views created didactic poetry in Korea, and the same was true in other countries. In Europe they are identified as the first intellectuals.[11] They had a deep bond with the peasantry, and in some places with the bourgeois. The world view of vernacular didactic poetry is a joint work of the reasoning and experience of intellectuals and lower-class people. This is a typical instance that shows how changes in literary genres were related to the replacement of literature-creating groups.[12]

5

The periodization of the ancient, medieval, and modern ages obtains new meaning in my approach, which uses two tactics. One tactic is to start with Korean literature and continue on to East Asian literature and world literature. The other is to begin from linguistic history and move to the changes in literary genres and the replacement of literature-creating groups.

The former tactic can be changed according to the researcher's situation. One uses the literature with which one is familiar as a starting point for a broader view and deeper insight. But the latter is unchangeable in any case. The epistemological process going from known result to hidden cause is a reliable means to restore the relationship between literary history and social history.

There is no single key to understanding world literary history. The distinction between major literatures and minor literatures is mistaken. All literatures, in any place, made their own contributions to world literature. We have to make an unlimited effort to find the whole process systematically by comparative studies on a broader scale.

To advance the study of literary history to a desirable level, we have to go beyond national limits. Each nation's literature has to be understood as a part of the literature of a civilization. Furthermore, inter-civilizational comparative study is a better goal from which general theories can be formulated.

During the medieval age, the nations in the center, in the intermediate regions, and in the periphery of each civilization each played important roles. The literatures produced by nations in similar situations within their respective civilizations show remarkable homogeneity. There are many interesting themes for comparative study to be found here.

6

Roughly speaking, Korea and Middle Europe as the intermediates Japan and Scandinavia as the peripheries offer many interesting themes for close comparison. Japan and Scandinavia were the homes of the Waegu ("Wakou" in Japanese, "Wokou" in Chinese) and the Vikings, two forces of peripheric revolt. The fact that Japan and Scandinavia were promoters of vernacular literature might be closely related to this. Japanese gunkimonogatari can be compared to the Icelandic saga.

The divisions between the intermediate regions and the periphery vary. Among Scandinavian countries, Denmark is close to begin an intermediate. Denmark's search for identity in the common heritage of medieval Europe is similar to the Korean case.[13]

The Christian monk Saxo Grammaticus' Danish history

Gesta Danorum, written in Latin, has a good counterpart in Korea. The Buddhist monk Iryeon wrote the Korean history *samkukyusa* (*Memorabilia of the Three Kingdoms*) in classical Chinese at almost the same time during the late medieval age. These two authors insisted that there were glorious national histories based on mythical evidence before Christianity or Buddhism came and imposed a new order.

Mutual dependence as well as conflict between the religious universalism of the whole civilization and the national identity with original tradition are the principal subjects of these two historical writings. This can be understood as a typical intellectual orientation of intermediate countries. To formulate a general theory from this idea, broader examples from other civilizations must be examined.

Notes

[1] Seoul: Jisiksaneopsa. A single-volume abridged version has been published in French: Cho Dong-il et Daniel Bouchez, *Histoire de la littérature coréenne des origines à 1919* (Paris: Fayard, 2002).

[2] In *Société féodale* (Paris: Albin Michel, 1968).

[3] Marc Bloch's Europe is "Europe Occidental et Centrale" (*ibid.*, p. 15).

[4] The conception of diglossia is well defined and used in Francis Britto, *Diglossia, a Study of Theory with Application to Tamil* (Georgetown: Georgetown University Press, 1968). Tamil's case is similar to Korea's.

[5] The word "medievalization" is not found in the *Oxford English Dictionary* (Oxord: Claredon, 1987). But it must be used as a basic term equivalent to "modernization."

[6] I summarized the outline of Korean literary history in my book written in English, Cho Dong-il, *Korean Literature in Cultural Context and Comparative Perspective* (Seoul: Jipmoondang, 1997), pp. 7-30.

[7] To answer this question I wrote *Dongasiamunhaksa Bigyoron* (*A Comparative Study of East Asian Literary Histories*, Seoul:

Seouldaehaggyochulpanbu, 1993) and *Hanaimyeonseo Yeoreosin Dongasiamunhaksa* (*One and Many East Asian Literatures*, Seoul: Jisiksaneopsa, 1999).

[8] Régis Boyer, *Histoire des littératures scandinaves* (Paris: Fayard, 1996), pp. 39-57.

[9] In the case of Arabic it was oral didactic poetry, as there was no written literature. See Albert Arazi, *La réalité et fiction dans la poésie arabe ancienne* (Paris: G.-P. Maisonneuve et Larose, 1989).

[10] Immanuel Wallestern's terms "the center," "the semi-periphery," "the periphery" are the product of the center oriented prejudice. His opinion that the world system was created through capitalism reflects the modernist view of history.

[11] Jacques Le Goff, *Les intellectuels au Moyen Age* (Paris: Seuil, 1957).

[12] My theory of literary history explained in this paper is discussed in detail in many books written in Korean. *Gongdongmuneomunhakgwa Minjogeomunhak* (*The Literature of Common Written Language and the Literature of National Languages*, Seoul: Jisiksaneopsa, 1999), *Segyemunhaksaui Jeongae* (*The Development of World Literary History*, Seoul: Jisiksaneopsa, 2002) are the most important.

[13] Brian Pastrick McGuire ed., *The Birth of Identities, Denmark and Europe in the Middle Age* (Copenhagen: C. A. Reitzel, 1996).

Ⅳ

Historical Changes in the Translation from Chinese Literature: a Comparative View of Korean, Japanese, and Vietnamese Cases

1

Translation is a core means of developing human civilization. Human civilization can be defined as the total sum of the creative inventions of all nations or ethnic groups in the world. But such an idealistic view is denied by the fact that each nation or ethnic group uses its own language, which can not be understood by others. The only way to overcome the barrier, which hinders the unification of human wisdom, is translation.

Not only the verbal forms of cultural products, but also even material devices can be exchanged and accumulated as long as they are translated or explained by translation. In the framework of the history of translation, the main currents of the development of human civilization can be revealed. But a world history of translation has not yet been written and published. We are still so ignorant of ourselves.

In Europe, Henri Van Hoof's *Histoire de la traduction en occident* (Paris: Duculot, 1991) can be found. This book explains the histories of translation in France, England, Germany, Netherlands, and Russia, one by one, with many details. The author's erudition deserves admiration. But translation is an international process, each tradition intermingled with others among language groups. Partitioning them into national divisions unreasonably simplifies their complexity.

Now it is the time to try to formulate a dynamic theory of translation. Assembling data even on national levels can not solve the problems from a theoretical perspective. Both the study of translation as an independent discipline or translation studies within the field of comparative literature have until now been too microscopic to aid in understanding the vital structure of translation.

2

To find an intercultural, dynamic theory of translation, we must verify the cases of other civilizations beyond Europe. East Asian civilization can contribute much to this. But the actual situation is not encouraging. Translation studies in East Asia started late with a European influence, and are preoccupied mainly with the one-way importing of European literature into their respective nations.

The reason for such undesirable deviation is that those

scholars trained in Western academic societies engage in translation studies with the intention of alleviating the cultural shock they feel. The East Asian classics are hard to understand for them. The wider problems of translation among East Asian languages in the premodern age are beyond their ability.

The specialists of classical literature in each East Asian country sometimes produced precious works in translation studies. But they are unknown not only to the readers of Western languages but also to their compatriots studying modern literature. And the scope of the translation studies of the specialists of classical literature are limited to the relationship between two countries. The whole area of East Asian literatures has not come into the scope of modern scholarship.

Literary Migrations, Traditional Chinese Fiction in Asia (Beijing: International Culture Publishing Corporation, 1987), edited by Claudine Salmon, is remarkable. It provides a wide range of information about how traditional Chinese novels are translated in Asian countries, including Korea, Japan, Vietnam, Thailand, Malaysia, and Indonesia. Some outstanding papers by specialists in each country are presented in translation.

But it lacks a systematic view. There is no attempt to compare various cases to draw any general conclusions. The understanding of translation is too naive. China is the giver, and the other countries are the receivers. That is all. The problem of cultural interaction between the giver and the receiver is not considered.

To understand the case of the novel, we must think of its situation in the history of translation. The novel is the latest property of the translation from Chinese literature. So it must be compared with the previous classics. The history of translation has to be based upon improving, the periodization of literature, and contribute to improving it.

3

So I would propose a new study in this paper. It is not a finished work, but a study plan with hypothetic assumptions. As it is impossible for me to provide all the details necessary for this work, I want help from literary historians and comparatists of other countries. I very much desire to meet counterparts for an international cooperative study.

As a scholar studying Korean classical literature, I first worte *Hangukmunhaktongsa* (*A Comprehensive History of Korean Literature*) (Seoul: Jisiksaneopsa, 1982-1986) in five volumes, and then enlarged the main scheme for understanding literary history into *Dongasiamunhaksabigyoron* (*Comparative Study of East Asian Literary Histories*), (Seoul: Seoul National University Press, 1993). Now I am approaching the third goal, world literary history.

In *Segyemunhaksauiheosil* (*Fiction and Facts in Writing World Literary Histories*), (Seoul: Jisigsaneopsa, 1996), I criticized 38 kinds of world literary histories, written in 8 Western and Eastern languages. I also proposed some new theoretical perspectives for overcoming the Eurocentric prejudice in understanding world literary history.[1] This paper is a partial work to prove these perspectives.

Now what is needed above all is a macroscopic insight to understand the historical changes in the interaction between the unity and the variety of the literature on the civilizational level. In the medieval age, the unity of a civilization was supported by the common written language, while national vernacular languages promoted the variety. The interrelationship of these two aspects is the main point of my immediate research.

East Asia is a good example of a civilization which had a common written language in the medieval age. Translation from the literature of the common written language is the best indicator of the dynamics of a civilization. That is the reason why I selected the theme of this paper, "Historical Changes in the Translation from Chinese Literature: a Comparative Study of Korean, Japanese and Vietnamese Cases."

China, Korea, Japan and Vietnam were East Asian countries with a common heritage of medieval civilization. China was its center, and the other three were the peripheries that were influenced by the center, in terms of literary exchange as well as in other spheres of culture. But we must not think that the giver is superior and the receiver is inferior. The dynamics of the cultural hegemony were not so simple.

Korean, Japanese, and Vietnamese peoples regarded themselves as the legitimate heirs of the common heritage of classical literature. The literati of the three countries not only modified and recreated their borrowings from China, they also competed with their Chinese counterparts to make their own distinct cultural world within the broader framework of the same civilization.

There were continuous translations from Chinese

literature. But the characteristics of the translation changed according to the historical stages. Changing characteristics mean shifts in cultural interaction and hegemony.

4

In the first stage, ways of reading Confucian and Buddhist scriptures written in classical Chinese, using the linguistic devices unique to each nation, were invented. Vietnamese people learned Chinese under Chinese rule. But they read Chinese texts with Vietnamese pronunciation. Koreans and Japaneses also invented their own pronunciations to read classical Chinese.

The texts of classical Chinese read with Vietnamese, Korean, and Japanese pronunciations are not intelligible to Chinese. The visual aspect of the common classical language of East Asia confirms the unity of a civilization, the audial aspect its diversity. The term classical or written "Chinese" is inadequate, as it leads to misunderstanding of both aspects.

The Vietnamese convention of calling the common language of East Asian civilization "Han" is excellent.[2] It is an abridged form of the common term of the three countries, "hanvan" (in Vietnamese), "hanmun" (in Korean), "kanbun" (in Japanese). But in Chinese, "hanwen" means something else, namely Han dynasty prose. In this case, by majority rule, the Chinese term loses its qualification as the standard.

The literati of the three countries inherited their ways of understanding Han, the written language of East Asian civilization. And they did not study colloquial Chinese, as it was regarded as without value. Only small numbers of professional interpreters were trained to speak Chinese.

Sheol Chong, a scholar of the seventh century, is known as a forerunner in inventing the Korean method of reading Chinese texts. Japan seems to have adopted the same method. In Japan it is used even now, known as "kundoku." It is a way to read Han by translating it.

During the first stage, until about the twelfth or the thirteenth century, the important Han classics were understood well by Vietnamese, Korean, and Japanese men of learning. So the Han classics became the common property of East Asia. Each member of the civilization had the equal right to use them in their own way. The civil service examination system, which tested the ability to read and write the Han, was launched in Korea in 958, and in Vietnam in 1075.

In the second stage, Confucian and Buddhist scriptures and some important literary classics were translated into national languages. Vietnamese king Ho Quy Ly's translation of Confucian scriptures in the early fourteenth century marked the starting point of the new stage. The Korean alphabet, *Humninjeongeum*, invented in the fifteenth century, ably played the same role.

In Japan, the way of reading Han texts by translating them was used continuously. So it was sufficient for Japanese people to publish the texts with marks added for the Japanese way of reading. Editing Han texts with such marks was called "Kundai." *Tōshi Kundai* (*Poems of the Tang Dynasty in the Japanese Way of Reading*) is a good example.

Koreans abandoned such methods after inventing the

Korean alphabet. With the new writing system, well designed for representing Korean oral language, the three domains of Han classics—Buddhist scriptures, Confucian scriptures, and literary works—were widely translated. The second stage was clearly distinct from the first stage in Korea.

But in that period, the translated texts did not replaced the originals. These translations helped readers understand the classics and were published along with them in bilingual editions. The translations of Buddhist scriptures was rather freer than that of Confucian scriptures, as they were designed to be read even by women. In the case of the literary works, the style or expression of the Korean language used in the translation had to be an issue. So *Dusieonhae* (*Translation of Dufu's Poems*) offered some excellent examples of the beauty of Korean language.

5

In the third stage, a new genre of Chinese literature, the novel, became the favorite item for translation. The three other East Asian countries developed their own genres of the novel along with the Chinese one.[3] So the Chinese novel was not a classical model but a companion as well as a rival of the same age.

The novels of the four countries needed multiple exchanges of themes and techniques. But the Chinese novel was the giver, and the others were the receivers, as in the previous stages. The reason is that, given the linguistic situation, Chinese novels could be understood by the others, but the reverse was impossible. Translations among the other three countries are very limited because of language barriers even today.

Chinese novels, though they were popular literature, were written in classical Han. Some of them used a mixed style, adopting colloquial Chinese. But the literati of the other three countries who were trained in Han had no difficulty reading them.

As the novel was not a classic, it was translated freely and adapted widely. There was no concept of copyright. Nor was there any distinction between the translation and the creation. Korean, Japanese, and Vietnamese novels increased rapidly owing to the active importing of ideas and motifs. What they received was not decided by the giver. Three countries showed their own tastes in selection and transformation.

In Korea, Chinese yanyi, or historical novels, were particularly popular. *Sanguozhiyanyi* (*The Romance of Three Kingdoms*), by Luo Guanzhong, was read the most widely and had much influence. There were original works with many complete translations, partial translations, partial translations with additional adaptations, rewritings, and works using its motifs.

The favorite work in Japanese was *Shuihu Zhuan* (*Water Margin*). Its Japanese translation, *Suikoden*, produced many adaptations, such as *Honchō Suikoden* (*Our Country's Suikoden*). In Vietnam, the adaptations of *Xiou Ji (The Pilgrim to the West*) enjoyed much popularity.

Some novels, which were judged to be masterpieces, adopted Chinese sources effectively in discussing their own social problems. The Korean *Cheonsuseok* (*Spring, Water, and Stone*), the Japanese *Nansō Satomi Hakkenden (The Story of Eight Warriors Named Dogs of the Satomi Family in Nanso Province*), and the Vietnamese *Kim Van kiew* (*Mr. Kim and Van-Kiew Sisters*) are such works. They showed the culmination of the East Asian premodern novel.

The unknown author of *Cheonsuseok* borrowed the historical background and some minor characters from Luo Guanzhong's historical novel *Cantang Wudai Yanyi* (*The Romance of the Remained Tang and Wudai Period*). It vividly depicted the fact that every traditional value was shaken as the vast Tang Empire collapsed. But there is no catastrophe for those who understand the inner process of historical change and join in a new start. Such a theme was used, I think, to suggest the author's philosophy of overcoming medieval society.

Nansō Satomi Hakkenden was a major work of an outstanding Japanese professional novelist, Takizawa Bakin (1767-1848). During the long period from 1814 to 1842, he worked diligently to write a long masterpiece, even losing his sight. He brought together every precious and astonishing thing he could think of. Adopting some plots from the most important rival work, *Shuihu Zhuan*, was indispensable. That made his novel colourfully and wonderfully interesting. He interposed in the novel several manifestations, written in classical Han, to announce his ambitious ideas to make an unprecedented novel.

Vietnamese writer Nguyen Du (1767-1820), during a diplomatic mission to China from 1813 to 1814, found the Chinese novel *Jin Yuan Qiao Zhun*(*Mr.Jin and Yun-Qiao Sisters*), and translated it into Vietnamese while freely adapting it. As he used a Chinese setting, it was possible to depict the decayed society vividly from a critical perspective. His inner message of lamenting the lost hope of a people's revolution was expressed through the story of a heroine who could not forget her lost love, lived as a prostitute, and was sacrificed by the cruel violence of merciless fate.

6

The three stages in the historical changes in the translation from Chinese literature were almost the same in Korea, Japan, and Vietnam. The three stages can be identified as the early medieval age, the late medieval age, and the transitional period from the medieval to modern ages. The peripheral countries began to approach the universal civilization in the early medieval age, made it their national property in the late medieval age, and finally opened wide the polycentric directions of literary creation in the transitional period from the medieval to modern ages.

Similar stages of the historical changes in the translation from the literature of the common written language can be identified in other civilizations. Not only East Asian civilization but also Sanskrit, Arabic, and Latin civilizations experienced the same process of transformation from the early medieval age to the transitional period from the medieval to modern ages.

The changes of the characteristics of translation from the literature of common literary languages to the national literature is sufficient proof to formulate a theory of the universal periodization of the literary history of the world. To prove such hypothetic assumptions, comparative studies covering wide ranges of human history are needed.

Notes

[1] Its outline is presented in an article, "Toward a new periodization of world literary history" in my book *Korean Literature, in Cultural Context and Comparative Perspective* (Seoul: Jipmoondang, 1997). It was presented originally at the congress of "Comparative Literature in Arab World" held at Cairo University, 20 December 1995.

[2] Its usage is easily identified in the books written in Western languages and published in Vietnam. Nguyen Khac Vien et al., *Vietnamese Literature* (Hanoi: Foreign Languages Publishing House, date unkwown) is a good example.

[3] The Korean term for the novel was "soseol" (minor saying), which came from China. Its meaning was redefined according to the actual characteristics of Korean novel. The Japanese term commonly used was "gesaku" (playful composition). The emphasis on pleasure is reflected in the term, as Japanese novels developed as favorite articles of commerce. The Vietnamese novel "tryennom" (tale in popular script) was written in verse.

From Oral to Written Epics: Toward a Comparative Study of Asian and African Cases

1

Here I am in Africa. As a scholar of comparative literature especially interested in oral literature, I have wanted for a long to time to have the opportunity to experience and join directly in the discussion of the African tradition of the oral epic. The oral epic, one of the most archaic and enduring types of oral literature, can open a new horizon in the understanding of world literary history. Africa is not only the home of the human race, but that of the oral epic as well, and the fact that the 16th congress of the ICLA is being held in Africa is good news to all sincere scholars who are seeking the true history of the epic.

But looking over the programme of the congress, I was disappointed to find only a few papers on African oral literature, and none on the oral epic. It makes me wonder whether South Africa is Africa, and whether or not the notorious apartheid has been abolished in the field of literary study. Almost all the papers presented during this congress have been selected to demonstrate European discourses. Fashionable epithets, such as "postcolonial," "multicultural," and "global," in the titles are merely empty clichés, as there is no sincere desire to study African and other Third World literatures in their original contexts.

Apartheid in academic study is not overcome through a political struggle, but by logical counterargument supported by sufficient evidence. The postcolonial theory of literature must be formulated on a global scale through true multicultural studies. Crucial to this is the cooperation of Asia and Africa in the comparative study of oral literature before the impact of Europe.

2

The assumption that the true epic can be found only in European literature, especially in the works of Homer, is false. Such Eurocentricism hinders our understanding of world literary history as it really is. We must move away from the fixed conception of the epic and examine the wide range of variations and transformations in this genre, accepting the various heritages of the many cultures around the world.

For the purpose of our study, let us select some intact examples that attest to the living history of the epic. Greek examples are deformed, as they are only written epics of ancient times. The endeavor to find its lost partner, the oral epic, in the Serbo-Croatian tradition did not produce any convincing results. The interrelation of oral and written epics, as well as the transformation of the written epic, can best be investigated through materials found intact in many parts of Asia and Africa. A comparative study of these two cases will offer a fresh new approach to world literary history.

The oral epics that maintain the ancient ways of thinking are the best starting point for the study of the epic's world history. Such precious treasures have been preserved to this day in Asia by the Ainu, some minorities of China, and the Korean people. The epics *Mwindo* and *Sunjata* occupy the same place in Africa. Some epics, such as the Mongolian *Jangar*, the Tibetan *Gesar*, the Korean *Barigongju* (*Abandoned Princess*), and the Egyptian *Hilali* reflected in their transmission the changing consciousness of the masses and became popular literature of the medieval era.

The rich heritage of the oral epic produced its written successor. The written epics, which adhered to an orthodox medieval ideology, were composed at a certain time to announce the coming of a new age. The Korean epic *Yongbieocheonga* (*Songs of Flying Dragons*) and the Swahili epic *Heraklios* are good examples. In modern times, new epics are written to inspire nationalism. African poems praising Chaka's heroic struggle against colonialism have their counterparts in modern Korean epics.

The long history of Asian and African epics plays a vital role in promoting discussions about the direction in which contemporary society is headed. With its foundation in oral tradition, the epic provides us with the creativity and imagination needed to overcome the Eurocentric model of modern literature and to open up a new age in world literary history.

3

I published a book titled *Dongasiagubiseosasieui Yangsanggwa-byeoncheon* (*Aspects and Changes of the East Asian Oral Epics*, 1997). It is not only the first systematic study of the East Asian oral epic, but also a new attempt to draw a world map of the epic tradition. It is regrettable that the book is written in Korean—and there is no translation—but writing in Korean is advantageous, since I can use Korean terms and framework.

I call the object of the study "seosasi." "Seosa" means "narrative," while "si" means "song." The Korean term "seosasi" designates all kinds of narrative songs, without any special cultural connotations derived from the ancient Greek epics. Using a term with such a wide meaning allows me to develop a comprehensive discussion. The term "epic" as used in this book is defined as the whole range of narrative songs, both heroic and non-heroic. The areas covered are as follows:

(1) Jeju Island, Korea
(2) Mainland Korea
(3) The Ainu, Ryukyu, and Manchurian peoples, and the minorities of Southwest China
(4) China, Japan, Vietnam
(5) Mongolia, Tibet, Kirgiz
(6) Philippines, Thai, Tamil, Rajastan
(7) Nyanga, Hawaii, Quiche, Babylonia
(8) The entire world

This divisions are basically concentric circles, starting at the core of Jeju Island, Korea, and developing gradually to the outer circle of the entire world. As the scope is widened, the accuracy decreases. Although an African example, the Nyanga epic *Mwindo,* is used, the African case is only partly covered as a distant view.

The core is the important part. From the Korean case, including Jeju Island and mainland Korea, I have drawn the following three main categories of the oral epic: '1. The epic of the god,' '2. The epic of the hero,' and '3. The epic of the commoner.' These three categories are further divided into seven subcategories: '1.1. The laudatory epic,' '1.2. The creation epic,' '2.1. The epic of the female hero,' '2.2. The epic of the male hero,' '3.1. The god-degrading epic,' '3.2. The hagiographic epic,' and '3.3. The lovers epic.'

1.1. and 1.2. are rooted in the primitive age, 2.1. and 2.2. are the epics of the ancient age, and 3.1., 3.2., and 3.3. are all products of the post-medieval world. The heritage of the written epic is also rich in Korea. Types 1.1. and 3.3. appear often in written form in classical Chinese as well as in Korean. Nowadays, Korean poets are eager to write national epics.

The categories drawn from Korean epics (K) are also found in the traditions of other East Asian peoples. The above-mentioned types are distributed as follows among the Ainu of Japan (A), the Ryukyuan of Japan (R), the Manchurians of China (M), and the minorities of Southwest China (SW):

	K	A	R	M	SW
1.1.	+	+	+	+	+
1.2.	+	+			+
2.1.	+				
2.2.	+	+	+	+	+
3.1.	+			+	
3.2.	+				
3.3.	+	+			+

The Ainu version of type 1.1. is the most archaic of the five examples. There is much similarity between Korea and the minorities of Southwest China in type 1.2.. Type 2.1. is not found outside of Korea, while 2.2. is quite common and widespread. The heroic life pattern is particularly well manifested in the Korean and Ainu examples. The Korean version of type 3.1. is quite similar to the Manchurian version, even down to the details. No other Asian peoples possessed type 3.2., while type 3.3. flourished among the Koreans and the minorities of Southwest China.

The general process of the epic's transformation, from the primitive, through the ancient and medieval, and into the early modern period, can be reconstructed through a historical typology. Each people show certain aspects of this process. In Korea, the continuity and the change in the whole range of epic history is very clearly defined.

China and Japan are not shown in the chart, primarily because there are no noticeable epics in their literary histories. The reason for this may be found in their conquering and assimilation of other peoples, which may have caused them to lose their own substrata of oral tradition, the wellspring that offers a continuous renewal of the written epic. The peoples threatened by imperial China and Japan protected their oral epics as symbols of national pride. The oral epic is the opposite of the state of political hegemony. Korea occupied the intermediate position, connecting and unifying the oral tradition with the written creation as she succeeded in developing a nation-state in the face of foreign aggression.

4

Now I want to compare the Asian cases with African cases. The title of this paper reflects a hope, in that the comparison of the two cultures cannot be carried out by a specialist from one side only, but demands a committed cooperation. So I have come here to Africa to understand the current academic state in Africa and to find a partner in this cooperative work.

The age of ignorance concerning the African epic, typified by Ruth Finnegan's *Oral Literature in Africa* (1970), has passed. The endeavor to defend the African epic using European criteria, as in Isodore Okpewho's *The Epic in Africa* (1979) is unconvincing. The rich heritage of the African oral epic must be investigated, sampled, and studied by indigenous investigators according to their own conceptions. So far, an abundant harvest of materials has been reported.

But, as I cannot read African language texts, I must rely on books written in European languages. *Oral Epics from*

Africa (1997), edited by John William Johnson et al, and Stephen Belcher's *Epic Traditions of Africa* (1999) are good guides reporting on the wide range of new knowledge. There are, however, some important problems to reconsider.

The view of *Oral Epics from Africa*, stating that "the variety of terms for long poetic narratives suggests that we need to redefine the notion of epic form from a global rather than a Western perspective" (p. xix) is good. It is the same with the East Asian cases I have investigated. Yet in the actual work of selecting and analyzing materials, I wonder whether or not the traditional African concepts are really used.

The two books classified their materials regionally, avoiding any participation in conceptional discussions. Such an irresponsible attitude only prolongs Eurocentric prejudice. Stephen Belcher's vague categorizations of the hunter's epic and the other epics, or his division of the mythical epic and the historical epic, cannot cover all the varieties of "long poetic narratives."

In order to overcome such confusion, it is recommended that the oral traditions within written works be compared. As revealed in Jan Knappert's *Epic Poetry in Swahili and Other African Languages* (1983), the Swahili epic 'utenzi' includes, in my terms, not only 'The epic of the hero' (*Liongo and Heraklios*), but also 'The epic of the commoner' (*Fatima*), without any discrimination between the two.

I think the whole range of the East Asian epic, defined as '1. The epic of the god,' '2. The epic of the hero,' and '3. The epic of the commoner,' has its counterpart in Africa. This is the true history of the epic, extending through the oral tradition and the written work. Europeans define the epic as 2. only and deny 1. and 3.. The reason is that they do not understand the connection between each type. Having lost the oral epic, they cannot understand the aspect of transformation in world literature.

The seven subcategories of the East Asian epic, '1.1. The laudatory epic,' '1.2. The creation epic,' '2.1. The epic of the female hero,' '2.2. The epic of the male hero,' '3.1. The god-degrading epic,' '3.2. The hagiographic epic,' and '3.3. The lovers epic,' may be common criteria for all of world literature. I would like to test this hypothesis through a comprehensive comparative study.

The fact that some peoples have all the epic types, while others have only some of them, and still others have none of them, can be explained, I think, by the ideas of maintenance and loss. A political power that conquers and assimilates often destroys its own precious cultural tradition. Overdevelopment causes collapse, while oppressed peoples recreate human wisdom on a higher level.

V

Mutual Understanding of Hagiographic Traditions

1

Does religion cause conflict or harmony? That depends on how and from what aspect one perceives religion. A new answer to this old question can be gained from a comparative study of hagiographies.

The exclusive dogmas of various religions can be the cause of long-standing conflicts. Such religion is maintained by orthodox scriptures and their authoritarian interpreters. The main content of the scriptures consists of episodes and teachings from the life of the founding father. He might have been a liberal thinker who wanted to remove the barriers of the former religion, but once he became the hero of the scriptures, everything became fixed.

Absolute truth was not to be questioned. Even the languages used in the scriptures were sacred. No one can change the fixed scriptures. Adding new experiences from later ages or other places is not permitted. Scriptural religions, rigorously applying the original theology to different situations, create conflicts not only between religions but also among believers of the same religion.

There is, however, another aspect of religion. This aspect is reflected in hagiographies. The religion of hagiographies is different from the religion of scriptures in many ways. The heroes of hagiographies are saints who are not fixed or limited. Hagiographies can be changed and supplemented. Any age or peoples may add their own saints. Any individual worthy of respect may become a saint. Hagiographies are typically regional products.

Hagiographies are religious as well as literary works. As they can be written or orally transmitted in various forms and recomposed in diverse ways, anyone can participate in creating and changing them. The religion of hagiographies is open and free. It transforms theology into folklore, philosophy into popular culture.

The theological doctrines fixed in the scriptures of the Christian, Islamic, Hindu, and Buddhist religions are mutually exclusive. But the stories in hagiographies do not conflict with each other. They can contribute to a harmony that is beyond the limits of each religion, and offer a common ideal for humankind.

Unfortunately, our knowledge of hagiographies has been very limited. Different peoples are only aware of their own religious and national heritage. We should broaden our views to foster mutual understanding and carry out multifaceted comparative studies.

2

The Christian hagiographies of medieval Europe offer a theoretical model for the comparative study of their conception, formation, and function.[1] Thus it is natural to begin our journey with the European case. The goal of comparative study, though, is to overcome a Eurocentric prejudice.

The best European Christian hagiographies are collected in *Legenda aurea* (*The Golden Legend*), written in the late 13th century by Jacobus de Voragine, an Italian monk. It contains the life stories of 164 Christian saints of various ages.[2] Eastern Europe, from the Byzantine Empire to Russia, also had a rich tradition of Christian hagiographies.[3]

Among the important protagonists of *Legenda aurea*, Saint Francis of Assisi is especially outstanding. His story begins as follows.

> He became a merchant and, until he was twenty years old, lived a vain and frivolous life. The lord chastened him with the whip of ill health and quickly made a different man of him, and he began to exhibit the spirit of prophecy.[4]

He then left home, renounced the world, became a wandering beggar, and practiced asceticism to seek the truth. He became a charitable man. He loved not only humble people but also all living creatures that were yet despised. It is said that "He preached to the birds and they listened to him," and that "He called all animals brothers and sisters."[5]

His actions are similar to that of a Buddhist monk. While Saint Francis was made a new man by his lord, Buddhist monks follow the same way voluntarily. It is astonishing that even the details of the story are similar.

The Tibetan Buddhist monk Milarepa is famous for being a saint who enjoyed a wondrous enlightenment after practicing severe asceticism. *The Life of Milarepa*, a biography written in the 15th century by Tsangyon Herika, one of his followers, is a precious classic of Tibetan literature. His poems are presented here and there in the book. I would like to quote some lines revealing his oath.

> Until I have attained *Siddhi*,[6] unto this solitude will I hold fast;
> Of starvation though I die, I'll not go to seek alms given in the faith or dedicated to the dead.
> For that would be to choke myself with dust.
> E'en though of cold I die, I'll not descend to beg for garments.
> E'en though of misery and sorrow I should die, I'll not descend to join in pleasures of worldly life.[7]

His reason for renouncing the world in such an extreme way is to save the world. After overcoming many difficulties, he became at last a spiritual teacher who would solve the disastrous problems of human life. His case is typical in a broad sense. Saints' lives presented by all other major religions consisted of the motifs of renouncing the world, practicing asceticism, attaining enlightenment, and saving the world.

3

In the Islamic world, "awaliya" or "auliya" means "friend of God." That term is equivalent to the word "saint." One who was called "sufi" was a member of the laity, not the clergy, but he had amazing experiences and became an intimate friend of God. Sufi stories are Muslim hagiographies.[8]

The Persian poet Farid al-Din Attar wrote a collection of Muslim hagiographies with the title, *Tadhirat al-Auliya (Memorials of the Saints).* One of the outstanding 75 saints included in this book is Abu Yazid al-Bestamini, a Persian *sufi*. His story says that he had a mystic encounter with God. After the experience he returned to ordinary life.

> 'A man encountered me on the road,' Abu Yazid recalled.
> 'Where are you going?' he demanded.
> 'On the pilgrimage,' I replied.
> 'How much have you got?'
> 'Two hundred *dirhams*.'
> 'Come, give them to me,' the man demanded. 'I am a man with family.
> Circle around me seven times. That is your pilgrimage.'
> I did so, and returned home."[9]

This story shows the means of his spiritual awakening. A meeting with God takes place once again in the lower world. The best pilgrimage is to give all one has to another who needs it.

The Indian word for the hero of a hagiography is "sant." The sant was known to have experienced ultimate truth through the devotional practice called "bhakti." They expressed such experiences in vernacular songs that could be easily understood. Kabir, Tulsidas, Surdas, and Mirabai are well known poet-saints.[10]

Such is the Hindi case. Other languages cherish the heritages of their own poet-saints. The Tamil tradition is particularly rich and proud; Appar, Campantar, and Cuntartar are worshipped widely and enthusiastically. Their songs are everlasting guides to spiritual awakening.[11]

Among Hindi poet-saints, Kabir receives special respect. His life story and his poetry offer deep inspiration to a wide range of people. During the 16th century, a devout admirer named Anananta-das wrote his life story in verse, *Kabir Parachai*. I would like to quote an impressive passage from it.

> He said: "Kabir, I have heard about you. For that
> reason, I have come to you."
> Hari had taken the form of an emaciated devotee. He
> requested cloth very humbly.
>
> When Kabir began to tear a cloth in half, Hari said:
> "Give me all of it, devotee, for I am naked."
> Kabir gave it to him immediately, without hesitation.
> Kabir did not return home.[12]

Kabir made a living with his family as a weaver, this being the caste into which he was born. If there was any profit, he used it all to feed others. One day the god Hari visited him in human form to test him. God fully proved the charity of Kabir.

4

Buddhist hagiographies appeared in India.[13] Other Buddhist countries developed their own traditions by adopting these hagiographies and adding new sources. Tibet was especially enthusiastic in this; hagiographies were the most precious part of Tibetan literature. We have already discussed one good example, the life story of Milarepa.

In North East Asian countries, Buddhism had to compete with Confucianism. Confucian historical records contain many biographies of important persons. Buddhist historians compiled "lives of eminent monks" ("gaosengzhun" in Chinese, "goseungjeon" in Korean, "kousouden" in Japanese). The word "eminent" was a conventional honorific title. These books were a kind of bibliographical dictionary. Materials concerning almost all known Buddhist monks were gathered in them.

The Chinese *Gaosengzhun* (*Lives of Eminent Monks*), written by Huijiao in the 6th century, initiated such a tradition. Among the books that followed, Zanning's *Gaosengzhun* (*Lives of Eminent Monks*), which deals with 656 persons, was the largest.[14] The Korean monk Gakhun wrote *Haedonggoseungjeon* (*Lives of Korean Eminent Monks*) using a literary style. The Japanese version, *Genkousyaksho* (*Buddhist Book of 1322*), compiled by Kokan Shiren included even non-Buddhist persons.

Most of the monks in these books conform to the desirable norms of religious life. Selfless ascetics dedicated to self-cultivation are praised. Sometimes, however, there are exceptional persons who break the rules. They wear rags, shout or sing with foul language, and even fall down drunk in the middle of the street. Through such behavior they are thought to tear down all kinds of fixed conceptions.

The story of Wangmin, a 9th century Chinese monk, in Zanning's book is particularly astonishing. "Wangmin" means "lost name". That is his name. He often took wine and meat and acted crudely in public. The following is the most remarkable episode of his strange behavior.

> One day he made a large cake. Calling his fellow monks, he said "let us go out for picnic to the graveyard." On the outskirts of the city there were many graves. People abandoned corpses there. He squatted on the ground and filled the cake with pieces of flesh from a rotting corpse. Putting it in his mouth, he swallowed it with pleasure. The other monks ran away, covering their noses and vomiting. He shouted. "If you eat this meat, you can eat other meat." The monks were suddenly enlightened.[15]

The graveyard is the world of the dead. It is also a working place of grave makers, the lowest people. He used it as a holy temple to gain enlightenment. Enlightenment is nothing but transcending the distinction between pure and impure, life and death.

Wonhyo, a Korean monk of the 7th century, is a

well-known hero of Chinese, Korean, and Japanese versions of *Lives of Eminent Monks*. His life was also a sequence of renouncing the world, practicing asceticism, attaining enlightenment, and saving the world, as it was with other Buddhist monks and the saints of other major religions.

At the same time, though, he was an exceptional person. He turned back while on his way to China to study Buddhism, realizing that the Buddha is in the mind. After he attained enlightenment, he married and became a layman.

The reason he did so is explained by interesting legends in Zanning's book. Pictures showing episodes from his life are national treasures of Japan. *Samgukyusa* (*Memorabilia of the Three Kingdoms*), a Korean historical record that includes many Buddhist hagiographies derived from oral sources, presents more meaningful stories.

> He met an entertainer who danced with a gourd mask, which he thought quite strange. He made his own gourd mask and called it "Unhindered," after a passage in the *Flower Garland Sutra* that says, "All unhindered men leave birth and death through a single path." He then sang this phrase until many people learned it. He toured thousands of villages, singing and dancing to convert the people, so that even the poor and ignorant knew the name of the Buddha, and to call on Amitabha in order to be born into his Pure Land.[16]

This story tells us more about Wonhyo's unusual way of enlightenment. He abandoned the scriptures and adopted a strange method of preaching, dancing and singing in the street. Through this he attested that the ultimate truth of religious idealism and the worldly life of humble, poor people are one in the same.

5

Were there any influences or adaptations among these saints or hagiographies? It is possible. Proof has been found that shows mutual relations between Muslim sufis and Hindu bhaktis. Kabir wanted to reconcile two religions. Such facts, however, can not explain the whole range of similarities. We must leave behind the diffusion theory in order to gain a deeper understanding of human civilization.

Humankind has a common ideal of an egalitarian community without privilege or prejudice. Such a view was well manifested in the medieval hagiographies of various religions. This was forgotten for a long time, though, as modern times presented a different set of values that placed winning above all else. Religions became the cause of conflicts.

To begin a new era, we have to reevaluate the message of harmony manifested in medieval heritages. The common ideal found in different hagiographies is a precious indicator for mutual understanding and cooperation in future. With it we can overcome the so-called clash of civilizations.

6

Hagiographies are the story of unusual saints who are not fixed or limited. Persons worthy of respect chosen by local criteria are freely added to them to realize humble peoples' desire for egalitarian society. They are typically regional products denying the centralist authority of religion and state.

They are transmitted as valuable heritages of popular culture. All peoples around the world can boast of and enjoy their own traditions through various ways of storytelling. The invention of animation and computer games has made them more interesting. Through developments in communication, hagiographies of different origins are able to be exchanged and shared widely.

Hagiographies can lead to an ideal pattern of globalization without one-sided dominance or hegemony. We can expect that they will help to overcome the so-called clash of civilizations and make a hopeful future. Hagiographic traditions are one of the best heritages of human civilization. Mutual comparison and general understanding of them are crucial tasks for the humanities and social sciences.

Notes

[1] Barbara Abou-El-Hj, *The Medieval Cult of Saints, Formations and Transformations* (Cambridge: Cambridge University Press, 1977), and Peter Brown, *The Cult of Saints, its Rise and Function in Latin Christianity* (Chicago: University of Chicago Press, 1982) offer a general introduction.

[2] Alain Boureau, *La légende dorée, le système narratif de Jacques de*

Voragine (Paris: Cerf, 1984).

[3] Hans-Georg Beck, *Das byzantinische Jahrtausend* (Münche: C. H. Beck, 1994); Jostein Bortnes, *Vision of Glory, Studies in Early Russian Hagiography* (Oslo: Solum Forlage, 1998).

[4] Jacobus de Voragine, William Granger Ryan tr., *The Golden Legend, Readings on the Saints* (Princeton, N. J.: Princeton University Press, 1993), vol. 2, p. 220.

[5] *Ibid.*, p. 225.

[6] This word refers to supernatural power.

[7] W. Y. Evans-Wentz tr., *Tibet's Great Yogi, Milarepa, a Biography from the Tibetan* (Oxford: Oxford University Press, 1969), p. 192.

[8] Henri Chamber-Loire et Claude Guillot dir, *Le culte des saints dans le monde musulman* (Paris: École Française d'Étrême-Orient, 1995).

[9] A. J. Arberry tr., *Muslim Saints and Mystics, Episodes from Tadhirat al-Auliya (Memorials of the Saints) by Farid al-Din Attar* (London: Routeledge and Kegan Paul, 1966), p. 114.

[10] R. D. Ranade, *Pathway to God in Hindi Literature* (Nimbal: Shri Gurudev Ranade Samdhi Trust, 1986); Karine Schomer and W. H. McLeod ed., *The Sants: Studies in a Devotional Tradition of India* (Delhi: Motilal Banrsidass, 1987); Vijay Mishra, *Devotional Poetics and the Indian Sublime* (Albany: State University of New York Press, 1998).

[11] Indira Viswanathan Peterson, *Poems to Siva: the Hymns of the Tamil Saints* (Delhi: Motilal Banrsidass, 1989).

[12] David N. Lorenzen, *Kabir Legends and Ananta-das's Kabir Parachai* (Delhi: Sri Satguru, 1991), p. 96.

[13] Reginald A. Ray, *Buddhist Saints in India: a Study in Buddhist Values and Orientations* (Oxford: Oxford University Press, 1994).

[14] These books are introduced in English by John Kieshnick, *The Eminent Monk: Buddhist Ideals in Medieval Chinese Hagiography* (Honolulu: University of Hawaii Press, 1997).

[15] Zanning's *Gaosengzhun,* volume 21, part 11.

[16] *Samgukyusa,* volume 4.

Biography and Confession: Eastern and Western Modes of Cultural Memory

1

It is a common desire of the human race to leave cultural memories using some kind of narrative form. Among these various heritages, the highest one is the mode of the final judgment of human conduct. It is chosen according to religious traditions.

Eastern Confucianist society and Western Christian society each have their own mode: the biography for the former, the confession for the latter. These two archetypes of the life history have been handed down, with modifications, over the long course of literary history. They can help to explain many of the contrasting features of the literary products of the two civilizations.

The formal biography, written as a part of the official historical records of the Eastern nations, following Sima Qian's model, decided a man's honour or dishonour, which are then passed on to his descendants. This is the last judgment of Confucianism. The historian must be fair and impartial; the readers of later generations will judge his sincerity. All other forms of biography are advised to follow such a norm. Any life history without the objective third person point of view is unacceptable; autobiography is not allowed.

In Western civilization, the highest mode of the life history is the religious confession to God, who judges the confessor's conduct-Augustine best exemplified this form. There is no other way to get to Paradise. The writer must be honest; God does not forgive any lie. In later modifications, the receiver may not be God himself, but the first person narration revealing an undisguised inner truth is retained. It is desirable for all distinguished persons to write an autobiography.

2

The East Asian novel began as a mock biography. It was a fictitious story of a humble person who was not qualified to be treated in the formal biography. Assuming the place of the biography, this enfant terrible registered its birth illegally, and started to destroy from within the declining medieval civilization.

The first novel in Europe, the picaresque novel, was a mock confession. It was a non-religious confession producing social disorder. The confessor was a swindler ("picaro" in Spanish) who boasted of his evil deeds under the pretext of begging pardon for them. The receiver was changed into an ordinary social leader.

The main concern for the two rising novels was the love affair. The secularizing society of the transition from the medieval to the modern era wanted such a interesting story. This story was embodied differently in the framework of two modes of cultural memory. The basic structure of the two novels showed an interesting contrast, and each modified a common tradition.

In East Asia, the polygamous novel was popular. It revealed the life history of a dignified man making love to many female partners. Such a situation helped to gain wider support for the mock biography. Whether the female characters were also interesting or not is different according to each work.

One Japanese example, Ihara Saikaku's *Koshokuichaio-toko* (*The Life of an Amorous Man*, 1682) was, as the title says, a man's story. The male protagonist pursued his adventure of sexual love unilaterally. There was no mention of the life histories of the female partners; they were expendable commodities.

A Chinese novel with a similar theme by an unidentifiable author, *Jinpingmei* (*The Plum in the Golden Vase*, late 16th century or early 17th century), was not wholly dominated by the erotic male protagonist. The three female characters, whose names were revealed in the title, led their own lives. After the death of the tyrannical hero, the story continued for a while to tell of the women's fate.

In Korea, Kim Manjung's *Guunmong* (*Dream of Nine Clouds*, 1687) was a life history of nine characters introduced as the nine clouds in the title. They are one husband and his eight wives. Such a relation can be labeled as unfair, but it was always the women who initiated the meetings for love in different ways, according to their social positions. Female readers could enjoy imagining themselves as each of the eight women.[1]

The Western counterpart of the Eastern polygamous novel was the so-called adultery novel. The polyandrous relationship, a love affair of a woman with two men or more, had a such a dishonourable name, but there is no decisive difference between the two. The multiple love affairs of polygamy or polyandry make for a more interesting story than monogamy. The two civilizations shared their choice.

The polygamous novel of East Asia was a biography or a series of biographies, so it used the third person point of view without exception. The adultery novel, however, used the first person point of view to confess the suffering of the inner mind. The recipient of the confession was changed into the lover; the lover became a new idol, love a new religion. Female readers ardently welcomed such a novel.

Its representative example, Jean-Jacques Rousseau's *Julie ou la nouvelle Heloïse* (*Julie or the New Heloise*, 1761) is a collection of letters. Two desperate lovers, who could not realize their love because of social barriers, exchanged endless letters repeating unbearable laments. What is important is only the inner consciousness. There is no noticeable development of the story, and only the death of one lover brings it to an end.

This sort of epistolary novel was the rearranged confession of the new age. It became fashionable in all of Europe and produced many variations. Its English representative, Samuel Richardson's *Pamela* (1740), which was mistakenly received as the founding father of the novel, was an exceptional "happy ending" story. The female protagonist succeeded in making the recipient read her letters and marry her.

Johann Wolfgang von Goethe's *Die Leiden des jungen Werthers* (*The Sorrows of Young Werther*, 1774) returned to the tradition of useless confession. The recipient of the desperate letters, however, is not a beloved idol but a third person confidant. The protagonist's death is not the convincing result of a failed love, but the beginning of a novel of inexplicable inner complex.

3

The modern East Asian novel received much influence from European precedents. Its traditional mode, however, was not lost but recreated. The family novel appeared as a new form of objective biography. It treated the social problem of historical change to the modern age.

The representative examples of such family novels were Shimazaki Toson's *Ie* (*Family*, 1912) in Japan, Ba Jin's *Jia* (*Family*, 1931) in China, and Yeom Sangseop's *Samdae* (*Three Generations*, 1931) in Korea. They treated a common theme, the death of the patriarch, and through this theme showed the same historical change from traditional to modern society. The specific features of each, however, differed according to each country's situation and each author's way of thinking.

The three novels agree that the death of the patriarch

cannot be stopped or delayed, as it is an inevitable process of the historical change from traditional to modern society, from authoritarian to democratic values. But the characters of the patriarch are different. In Shimazaki Toson's *Ie* he is a leader of peasants, in Ba Jin's *Jia* he is a member of the Chinese gentry who achieved his privileged status through the civil examination, and in Yeom Sangseop's *Samdae* he is one who achieved his position in the Korean gentry, the yangban, by money.

There are two types of successor: the moderate successor, who regrets the death of the patriarch, and the revolting successor, who welcomes it. The successor in Shimazaki Toson's *Ie* is moderate. the successor in Ba Jin's *Jia* is revolting, and in Yeom Sangseop's *Samdae* there are both moderate and revolting successors.

The moderate successor in Shimazaki Toson's *Ie* wants to inherit the fading Japanese tradition in order to overcome the impact of the West. The revolting successor in Ba Jin's *Jia* adopts Western liberalism to be free from patriarchal despotism. Yeom Sangseop's *Samdae* depicts the complicated conflict of Western liberalism, Communism, and conservatism among various successors.

The European novel had a similar work. Roger Martin du Gard's *Les Thibaut* (*The Thibauts,* 1922-1936), in France, depicted the death of the patriarch and showed a competition between the rightist way of the moderate successor and the leftist way of the revolting successor. But it is regarded as an outmoded work and standing outside the main tradition of the European novel of the 20th century.

The European novel was inclined to the stream of

consciousness. Its models, Marcel Proust's *A la recherche du temps perdue* (*In Search of Lost Times,* 1913-1927) and James Joyce's *Ulysses* (1922), receive ever increasing attention. They are new forms of the confession where the recipient is oneself. There is no lover or confidant; communication beyond oneself is impossible. It is the inner monologue in its literal sense.

The critical comment about such novels, that "even the most painstaking analysis can hardly emerge with anything more than an appreciation of the multiple enmeshment of the motifs but with nothing of the purpose and meaning of the work itself,"[2] is convincing. But it cannot change the situation. There is no alternative but to follow the course already chosen.

Franz Kafka and some other novelists destroyed the novel once more. At last, the so-called "nouveau roman" or "anti-roman" appeared. This is a final assault on the novel. The story is disturbed, the character is disintegrated, and historical consciousness has disappeared. There seems to be no remedy for the crisis of the novel.

New models of European literature were always highly evaluated by East Asian literary critics with a background in Western learning. They advised writers to imitate them. But the epistolary novel was not adapted as a fixed form, and experiments in writing stream of consciousness novels produced no noticeable results.

Confession without religious faith brought about the crisis of the European novel, but it is not a crisis of world literature. The tradition of biography, East Asia's mode of cultural memory, is still valid in secular and modernized society. East

Asian novels continue to depict history using third person point view.

The Japanese "watagushi shosetsu" ("I" novel) uses the first person point of view, but it does not destroy the novel. Historical novels on a large scale are very popular in Japan and Korea. Chinese and Korean novelists are eager to narrate modern social and political history better than the historians.

At first, the novel was a mock biography, but now it is a new form of the formal biography of society. The novel of mock confession can not be labeled as hopeless. If it can avoid too extreme an orientation, it will be able to offer a sincere testimony of human experience.

The East Asian mode of cultural memory emphasizes the outer side. While life in the family, community, and nation are highly valued, the individual's inner consciousness is relatively neglected. To unite the outer and inner orientations is the best method to improve cultural memory.

4

Just as the European sense of superiority is harmful, the East Asian insistence of self-righteousness is also wrong. Yet there are more than just two civilizations on the earth, and each civilization has its own mode of cultural memory. Comparative study in a wider scope will help overcome any kind of ethnocentrism.

Indian and Arab civilizations do not forget their glorious histories. The peoples without a written heritage must also not be neglected. Among them, I will select Africa to discuss the relation between the traditional mode of cultural memory and the modern novel.

Kenyan novelist Ngugi wa Thiong'o said that the European novel died with the death of God, but the African novel is still alive. "There was even a movement in search of *noveau roman* but I am not sure whether there was also a parallel movement in search of a new God or, for that matter, whether the search was fruitful." This is the European situation. "What's clear is that something answering to the name 'novel' has been showing significant signs of life somewhere in Africa and Latin America."[3] This is the other side of the story.

It is a well-known fact that the African novel was born as an imitation of the European model. Then why it does not have the same life cycle? The answer is that Africans did not believe in the European God but in their own myth.

The European God produced its peculiar mode of cultural memory, the confession. The death of God is well manifested in the decay of the confession in the novel. But the African mode of cultural memory is the myth and other oral folk narratives. African myth does not die, since it is a continuous prophecy concerning history.

The African novel is a union of its own tradition and the imported model. Its own tradition refuses to fade away and continues to protest against imperialism. Its mythical imagination goes beyond factual description of African tragedy and seeks a hopeful future. The Latin American novel has a similar orientation.

The European novel is not an obstacle. It has helped in

the investigation of the psychological side of the historical problem. Minute insights into the inner complex, received from European novel, are used well. Even the technique of the inner monologue produces appropriate effects. So the African novel has a better organization than the East Asian novel. It opens a third way to successfully unite the different modes of cultural memories.

If all civilizations on the earth were to exchange their merits in an egalitarian fashion, human wisdom would be greatly increased. This is the way to avoid the clash of civilizations and to realize the harmony of civilizations. Whether the new millenium is hopeful or not depends on our efforts.[4]

Notes

[1] Cho Dong-il, "Male-Female Partnership and Competition for the Classical Novel," *Korean Literature in Cultural Context and Comparative Perspective* (Seoul: Jipmoondang, 1997), p. 91.

[2] Erich Auerbach, Willard R. Trask tr., *Mimesis, the Representation of Reality in Western Literature* (Princeton: Princeton University Press, 1971), p. 551.

[3] Ngugi wa Thiong'o, *Decolonizing the Mind, the Politics of Language in African Literature* (London: James Currey, 1981), p. 64.

[4] This paper is a partial summary of my book written in Korean, *Soseolui Sahoesa Bigyoron vol. 1-3* (*A Comparative Social History of the Novels*) (Seoul: Jisiksaneopsa, 2001).

저자: 조동일(趙東一)
1939년 경북 출생
서울대학교 불문학과 · 국문학과 졸업, 문학석사, 문학박사
계명대학교 · 영남대학교 · 한국정신문화연구원
서울대학교 인문대학 교수를 거쳐 현재 계명대학교 석좌교수
『한국문학통사』『동아시아문학사비교론』『세계문학사의 허실』
『한국문학의 갈래이론』『삼국시대 설화의 뜻 풀이』
『한국문학이해의 길잡이』*KOREAN LITERATURE IN CULTURAL CONTEXT AND COMPARATIVE PERSPECTIVE* 등 저서 50여 종

한국학연구총서 33
한국 · 동아시아 · 세계문학 관련 논점 값 12,000원

2006년 5월 1일 1판 1쇄

저 자 조 동 일
발행인 임 삼 규
발행처 **지 문 당**

413-756 경기도 파주시 교하읍 문발리 514-7
등 록 1997. 12. 30. 제 1-2268호
영 업 부 (02)743-3192~3 팩스(02)742-4657
전자우편 sale@jimoon.co.kr
편 집 부 (02)743-0227 팩스(02)743-3097
전자우편 edit@jimoon.co.kr
홈페이지 www.jimoon.co.kr

ISBN 89-88095-98-7